HEY DAD, WANNA PITCH TO ME?

Helpful Hitting Tips for Kids

by Jim and Nick Hughes

**Front cover art and art within instructional chapters was drawn by the very talented
Curtis Dopson of Merrimack, New Hampshire.**

All comments of advice and encouragement were provided to James and Nicholas Hughes by each respective player and are direct quotes, except in cases where editing was necessary for form and content.

Copies of this book, as well as **Hey Dad, Wanna Play Catch?**, the first book in this series, may be purchased on-line at *www.heydad.org*, *www.hollispublishing.com*, as well as internet booksellers. Discounts are also available for groups.

ISBN 0-9746272-0-8

Printed by Puritan Press, Inc., 95 Runnells Bridge Road, Hollis, NH 03049, 603-889-4500, *www.puritanpress.com*

Dedication

This book is dedicated to Karen Hughes

Special Thanks

Special thanks to NH Grizzlies Baseball, Coach Mike Jackson, and Connie Jackson for their assistance and use of the Grizzlies batting cages. The NH Grizzlies are the oldest AAU baseball club in New Hampshire. Its main focus is instruction with a strong emphasis on pitching and hitting.

NH Grizzlies Baseball Club
64 Cutler Road
Litchfield, NH 03052

Thanks to Scott Campbell, Kyle Doolan, Taylor Bronson, Craig Duggan, Jack Kelley,
Adam Belcher and Nick for assisting with the demonstration photos.
Thanks also to Russ and Liz Belcher for their assistance.

A Helping Hand For Those In Need

A portion of the proceeds from the sale of this book will be donated to the Association of Professional Ball Players of America. Since 1924 they have provided financial assistance for those professional baseball players, coaches, umpires, scouts and clubhouse men who are in need. Much of their assistance involves cases of older, retired players who have been ravaged by illness and the infirmities of old age.

A.P.B.P.A.
1820 W. Orangewood Avenue, Suite 206
Orange, CA 92868

From the Authors

In our first book, "Hey Dad, Wanna Play Catch?" we covered some of the baseball fundamentals that every youngster should learn and practice in order to become a better player. These fundamentals covered many aspects of the game. They were combined with advice and encouragement from 99 former Major League Baseball Players to give the reader an insight into what it takes to be a professional ballplayer.

In this book we will concentrate on just hitting. It has been said that hitting a baseball well, is the single most difficult skill to master in sports. Most baseball players know the frustration of swinging at a bad pitch or striking out. To hit well, a ballplayer needs to know the proper mechanics involved in the swing, and practice as much as possible.

We will build on the batting fundamentals that were covered in "Hey Dad, Wanna Play Catch?" by concentrating on the different aspects of hitting, keys to becoming a better hitter, and drills that can be used to improve your hitting. Included in each chapter are tidbits of advice from former Major League ballplayers. These ballplayers were kind enough to share with Nick and me, a piece of advice that they thought might be helpful to young ballplayers. They all answered the question, ***What piece of advice would you give to a youngster, which you found to be helpful to you in your career?***

You should keep in mind that, just like any other aspect of sports or life in general, if you want to improve, it takes commitment and practice. Few people, are born with the natural ability to master the art of hitting. The secret is to do it correctly and to learn and practice the fundamentals. As you read the book, look for ways in which you can improve your hitting. Use some of the drills, outside in your yard or with your friends. Read the advice that these former ballplayers have given to Nick and me. We are confident that you will find ways to make yourself a better hitter.

Jim and Nick Hughes

Table of Contents

Foreword by Phil Rognier ix

Chapter 1 The Mechanics of the Swing 1
Mike Sandlock {Brooklyn Dodgers} 11
Jim Delsing {St. Louis Browns} 12
Johnny Hopp {Boston Braves} 14
Don Gutteridge {St. Louis Cardinals} 16
Johnny Blanchard {New York Yankees} 17
Alvin Dark {Oakland Athletics} 18
Mace Brown {Pittsburgh Pirates} 20

Chapter 2 The Mental Aspects of Hitting 21
Rick Wise {Boston Red Sox} 28
Al Pilarcik {Kansas City Athletics} 29
Billy Hitchcock {Philadelphia Athletics} 30
Johnny Lucadello {St. Louis Cardinals} 31
Jerry Kindall {Team USA} 32
Pete Coscarart {Brooklyn Dodgers} 33
Al Worthington {Minnesota Twins} 34
Sam Chapman {Philadelphia Athletics} 36

Chapter 3 Bunting 37
Hal Naragon {Cleveland Indians} 42
Ted Lepcio {Boston Red Sox} 43
Tony Kubek {New York Yankees} 44
Ed O'Brien {Seattle Pilots} 46
Art Kenney {Boston Braves} 47
Jim Davenport {San Francisco Giants} 48

Chapter 4 Slumps 49
Chuck Hiller {San Francisco Giants} 52
Bob Schmidt {New York Yankees} 53
Bill Rogell {Detroit Tigers} 54
Wade Boggs {Tampa Bay Devil Rays} 56
Andy Seminick {Philadelphia Phillies} 57
Roy Nichols {New York Giants} 58
Bill Lee {Boston Red Sox} 60

Chapter 5 Hitting Drills 61
Whitey Kurowski {St. Louis Cardinals} 71
Spider Jorgensen {Brooklyn Dodgers} 72
Woody Jensen {Pittsburgh Pirates} 73
Billy Hunter {New York Yankees} 74
Johnny Sain {Boston Braves} 75
Frank Fanovich {Philadelphia Athletics} 76
Hal Jeffcoat {Chicago Cubs} 77
Mike Naymick {St. Louis Cardinals} 78

Index 79
My Autographs 80
Team Addresses 83

FOREWORD
BY PHIL ROGNIER

Hitting a baseball has proved to be the toughest skill to master in all of sports. The ability to hit a moving ball, thrown by a person who is intentionally trying to deceive the hitter, requires intense concentration, superb hand-eye coordination, hours of practice, and a certain amount of luck. Even after all of this, the ball may be caught by someone for an out. To solidify the case even more, the best hitters are successful only 3 times for every 10 times they bat. Ted Williams once said, "You must hit a round ball with a round bat, square." Sounds fun to me!

The keys to becoming a good hitter have been debated for years, but certain ones seem universal. Almost all agree that a hitter must have good eyesight. A player must be able to see the ball to hit it. Everyone who plays baseball, at any level, should have an eye exam every year. A second element is to believe that you can hit. A positive attitude and courage to go to the plate, knowing that you will hit the ball, not only conquers fear but increases focus. Thirdly, hard work and practice contribute to the development of muscle memory and proper hitting techniques. It requires hours of practice, with focus on solid fundamentals, to learn how to hit a ball properly and be successful at the plate. A good hitter must be able to see the ball, adjust to what it is doing, and then hit it. If you want to be a good hitter you must be willing to spend the time, develop a strong work ethic, and find someone who will work with you to reinforce your enthusiasm and assist you in accomplishing your goals.

Jim and Nick Hughes have written, "Hey Dad, Wanna Pitch To Me?" as a guide and training aid for young people who want to learn how to hit, will work hard, and most importantly, whose parents, coaches, or friends will take the time to help them achieve their goal. The key element in a child's development of any skill is empowerment, especially from parents and family. The combination of hard work, love and encouragement, patience, and persistence is immeasurable in the overall personal development of a youngster's socialization process. Moreover, the bonding which occurs during the process can be lifelong and strengthen family ties, create self-esteem and confidence, and be a great springboard for a happy and productive life. "Hey Dad, Wanna Pitch To Me?" is an excellent tool for youngsters and their parents to read together as a starting point in developing a "game plan" on how to hit a baseball and becoming lifelong "teammates" at the same time!

It is important that parents take an active approach and interest in their child's desire to play baseball or any other sport or activity. Positive reinforcement and participation not only supports youngsters emotionally, but empowers them to reach for higher goals and to learn new skills. The overall value of baseball is not as an end in itself, but as a process to learn life's little lessons. By actively participating in the game of baseball, youngsters learn many of the social skills and physical prerequisites of being a productive citizen, spouse, and parent. Moreover, with the support and positive encouragement of their parents, they will also relax, learn at a quicker rate, and develop a strong sense of family and love. And . . . they will have a whole lot of fun!!! Jim Hughes and his son Nick have provided an outstanding "launching pad" for you and your children to learn together, how to hit a baseball, learn tips of the game, and develop proper fundamentals. The drills and dialogue are easy to read and understand, and with hard work, will guide you in achieving your goals.

Moreover, Jim has compiled another outstanding group of former big league ballplayers who, in clear and understandable terms, have imparted excellent advice. Advice that they found to be helpful to them in their own careers. Having been in baseball and a "baseball nut" for over 50 years, I believe that "Hey Dad, Wanna Pitch To Me?" will provide you with a positive fundamental guide to hitting, a unique learning step in your socialization, and an integral ingredient in strengthening family bonds. Keep in mind that learning to hit a baseball is frustrating, but can also be a whole lot of fun . . . especially when you get that hit!

Phil Rognier

Phil Rognier has been a baseball coach and instructor for the past 40 years in all levels of developmental baseball. An author, mentor, trainer, businessman and baseball fanatic, Phil brings a unique and sensible approach to his training of youngsters in the game of baseball. He is currently a consultant to Rebound Sports Technology, the makers of SwingAway, an innovative baseball hitting device. He is also Executive Director of "First Swing," a nonprofit organization dedicated to assisting physically and financially challenged kids.

Chapter 1

The Mechanics of the Swing

Mike Sandlock
Brooklyn Dodgers

Jim Delsing
St. Louis Browns

Johnny Hopp
Boston Braves

Don Gutteridge
St. Louis Cardinals

Johnny Blanchard
New York Yankees

Alvin Dark
Oakland Athletics

Mace Brown
Pittsburgh Pirates

The Mechanics of the Swing

Hitting Fundamentals

1 To hit well, a ball player needs to know the proper mechanics involved in the swing, develop a good hitting technique and practice as much as possible. You cannot be a good hitter unless you dedicate yourself to practice hitting.

2 Every hitter has a different swing and different batters will find success with different techniques. These differences are mainly based upon body size and structure, experience, and training. The secret to your success will be to find a style that works for you.

3 Regardless of the style you choose, base it on the fundamentals:

- Study the pitchers (get a feel for the speed and what type of pitch they throw, etc.).

- Keep your eyes on the ball until the bat makes contact. Know the strike zone and get a good pitch to hit.

- Know the situation (count, score, runners, outs) and what you need to do.

- Be aggressive. The hitter should load and stride on every pitch and be up there thinking hit, hit, hit, so that he is ready to explode with the hips and hands if it is a strike.

- If the pitch is not a strike, don't swing!

4 The question for every hitter should not be: **Do I swing?** The question should be: **Do I stop my swing?**

The Squared Stance

1 The term "batting stance" refers to the position of the body and bat while waiting for the pitch. Some hitters may choose a slightly closed stance, while others may prefer a slightly open position. Either is acceptable.

2 The distance between a hitter's feet should also be up left to the personal preference of the hitter. Hitters with a wide stance should still have room to stride as the pitch is being delivered and the hitter with a narrow stance should be careful not to over stride. The key is comfort because comfort leads to confidence.

3 Usually for younger players the "Parallel" or "Squared" stance is recommended. This means that the hitter has both feet an equal distance from home plate and on a direct line with the pitcher, and with each other. The hitter's feet should be little more then shoulder width apart. Be sure to stay on the balls of your feet, not flat-footed. You should feel springy and ready for action.

The batting stance is the position of the hitter's body and bat while waiting for the pitch.
This hitter is in the "Squared Stance."

The Mechanics of the Swing

4 The hitter should be close enough to the plate so that he can comfortably reach down and touch the outside edge of the plate with the bat. This will insure that he can reach the outside pitch as well.

5 After the feet are positioned, the hitter's weight should be equally balanced between the front and back legs. Both hips and shoulders should be parallel to the ground. Hitter should have a slight bend in the knees. When you look down at your feet, your knees should be bent just enough to prevent you from seeing your ankles.

6 Your hands should be just off the back shoulder with the bat angled at about 45%.

7 Where you stand in the batter's box will depend mostly on the speed of the pitcher.

The Strike Zone

1 The strike zone is the area above home plate that extends from the hitter's knees to a point which is halfway between the hitter's belt and the top of the hitter's shoulders.

2 A pitch passing through any part of this area is a strike, even if the batter does not swing at it.

3 You should consider every pitch to be a strike until you are satisfied that it's not.

Hitters should be close enough to the plate so that they can touch the outside edge with the bat.

The proper batting stance.

The strike zone.

The Mechanics of the Swing

The Batting Grip

1 A relaxed grip (although not too relaxed) is the best all around approach mechanically.

2 Many suggest that you should always align the middle finger knuckles when gripping the bat. This is not a bad practice, but the hitter should stick with a grip that is comfortable.

3 Remember that your top hand is always your dominant hand. When you pick up the bat, lay the handle where your palm meets your fingers in your top hand, (a little more toward the fingers than the palm). Close the grip by rolling your fingers around the handle and bringing your thumb up to your top finger. Repeat this with the bottom hand, but slightly more toward the palm this time.

4 The hands should be together with no space in-between them.

5 Keep a loose grip. This gives you the range of motion necessary to hit any pitch without rolling over or locking yourself up. The hands and grip will naturally tighten when the pitch is on the way.

6 Do not rest the bat in the palms of your hands. The palm grip will cause you to "muscle up" on the ball. When you do this, it usually means that you are trying to hit the ball too hard, or too far.

1. In your top hand, the bat should be a little more toward the fingers than the palm.
2. The bottom hand should grip the bat slightly more toward the palm.
3. The hands should be together with no space in-between them.
4. Hold the bat loosely in curled fingers, not in your palms. The bat should NOT be squeezed.

The Mechanics of the Swing

The Open Stance

1 In the open stance, your front foot is moved farther away from the plate than your rear foot. Only 3 to 5 inches is necessary.

2 This opens up or turns the front of your body toward the pitcher. You will still stride toward the pitcher so try not to "pull-off" the ball by stepping away from the plate.

3 This stance gives you an advantage on the inside pitch and makes it easier for a hitter to get the bat on the ball.

The Closed Stance

1 In the closed stance, your front foot is moved a little closer to the plate than your rear foot. This closes or turns your body away from the pitcher.

2 When taking your stride forward, you will be still stepping toward the pitcher, but because this stance forces your shoulder to stay closed longer, your swing is actually delayed.

3 Hitters often use this stance when expecting an off speed pitch, to get better coverage of the outside part of the plate, to hit to the opposite field, and to keep from pulling the ball.

Remember:

Most of the time, you will "Step and Hit." This means that you will be taking a comfortable step forward with your front foot and adjusting your swing to the pitch location as soon as the ball is released.

Open Stance

Squared Stance

Closed Stance

The Mechanics of the Swing

Positioning The Bat

1 Hold the bat steady at a 45 degree angle. Don't hold it straight up or flat over your shoulder.

2 Hold the bat about 8 to 10 inches from your chest and back toward the catcher.

3 Keep the bat and your body still. Don't bounce around or sway back and forth.

Bat Selection

1 Many young hitters believe that a larger bat will give them a better chance to hit the ball. This is not true. A bat that is light-weight gives a hitter more control and quicker bat speed.

2 Try the "30 Second Drill." When selecting bats, hitters should pick up the bat with their strong hand (right hand for right-handed hitters). Hold the bat down by the knob and extend your arm out away from your body. Hold this position for at least 30 seconds. If the bat begins to feel heavy or your arm gets tired, you should consider choosing a lighter bat.

The Balance Drill

1 To determine whether a hitter has a solid stance, a coach or fellow teammate should firmly push the hitter in the shoulder area in an attempt to knock him or her off balance. If the hitter actually takes a step or two backwards after this friendly nudge, then it should be apparent to the hitter that the stance is not yet solid.

2 This exercise should be repeated until the hitter stays relatively stationary. Remember, good pitchers can usually identify good hitters just by observing their stance.

3 In addition to a solid stance, good hitters will always stand on the balls of their feet before, during, and after the swing. If hitters are flatfooted, they will sacrifice a significant amount of power.

Remember:

Balance is necessary throughout the entire swing. It helps hitters to control their bat and body.

The proper bat position.

The balance drill should be used to make sure that the hitter has a solid stance.

The Mechanics of the Swing

Load

1 Many young hitters swing the bat after the ball is past them, and many times this happens because they don't get into the "load position" in time. "Load position" refers to the position that your body and bat need to be in just before the swing. All good hitters do this.

2 This phase is important because if done properly, it can help you make solid contact with the baseball on a more consistent basis.

3 Once the pitcher begins his movement forward with the pitch, you should then "load." The load position is the point where you have a comfortable, solid stance, and a good portion of your weight is on your back foot and leg. This involves a slight movement backwards (about 2 to 3 inches) of your hands, shoulders, hips and knees. Some hitters will actually raise their front foot and bring the entire leg back. Others will have just a slight recoil.

4 Either way, the hitter's weight shifts from a 50/50 front to back ratio, to a point where almost all the weight is on the back foot (usually a 40/60 front to back ratio). Maintain your balance.

5 During this load it is important that you keep your head steady and keep your eyes on the pitcher. Good hitters only use their front foot and leg to keep their balance before the pitch. It is also important that both knees be bent.

6 The upper body should be turned slightly or coiled like a snake in order to add even more power to the swing.

7 Your hands should be about shoulder high and back toward the catcher. The bat angle is about 45 degrees from the ground and not straight up or flat over your shoulder. Whether you hold your hands high or low, in toward your body or out away from your body, you will still need to get into the Load position from your starting position.

Remember:

Load before every pitch by shifting your weight onto your rear foot as the pitcher starts his movement forward with the pitch.

Around the time that the pitcher begins his movement forward with the pitch, the batter should lift the front leg up and back towards the catcher. Your body weight should be shifted towards the back leg. Use your front foot to keep your balance.

The Mechanics of the Swing

Stride

1 After you are in the Load position, you should be ready to make your movement toward the ball. This is called the stride.

2 The stride consists of a short step with the front foot directly towards the pitcher (5–7 inches), just as the pitcher is about to release the ball.

3 The stride should be a very soft movement of your front foot. You still want to keep your front shoulder in and your hands and weight back during your stride (Don't lunge at the ball). Picture it as stepping on thin ice. You don't want to put your whole weight on your front foot.

4 To generate as much power as possible at the point of impact, hitters should keep most of their weight above the back foot and leg when they stride.

5 It is important not to swing until your front foot has landed, because you want to hit against a firm front leg. When the front foot plants, the hitter will feel the power of their lower body exploding forward. Your bat, should be cocked and in the launch position.

6 The importance of the stride can be demonstrated with a simple exercise. Grab your bat and get in the hitting stance. Without moving your front foot, swing the bat as if you are about to hit a pitch. The result is an awkward, off balance type of motion made with your upper body. This creates little or no power and even if you hit the ball, it won't go very far. When you take this same swing using the load and stride, your hips and lower body help to generate the power and mechanics for a proper swing.

Remember:

Take your stride when the pitcher is just about to release the ball.

< As the pitcher releases the ball, the hitter should be striding towards the pitcher. The stride is no longer than 7 inches. The hitter should have the stride foot (front foot) down, well before the ball gets to home plate. Notice how weight stays over the back foot and leg. The bat should be in the launch position.

The swing involves bringing the bat forward and downward into the hitting zone. The knob of the bat should move toward the ball. >

The Mechanics of the Swing

The Swing

1 After you have completed your load and stride, you then begin the swing.

2 The first movement involves bringing the bat forward and downward into the hitting zone. The knob of the bat should move toward the ball.

3 The swing also involves rotating up on the ball of your back foot (this is known as squashing the bug).

4 The hips begin to rotate and the hands (bat knob) go toward the ball. If a player is truly hitting with his entire body, then the head of the bat will be the last to come through the hitting zone.

5 Your head should remain still with your chin going from your front shoulder to your back shoulder when finished with your swing.

6 Hitters should remember to keep their shoulders level as they swing. Dropping your back shoulder as you swing will cause you to swing up (uppercut) on the ball resulting in strike outs and pop ups. To avoid pulling your body and bat away from the strike zone during your swing, point your front shoulder toward the ball.

7 As your body starts to rotate, your top hand should be pulling the bat through the strike zone. At time of contact you want to have your bottom hand palm facing down and your top hand palm facing up. This will increase the chances of a line drive which provides you with the best chance of reaching base.

8 Your eyes should be focused on the ball. Make contact with the ball out in front of the plate. Swing through the ball and follow through after contact.

Remember:

- Knob of the bat toward the ball
- Rotate on the ball of your back foot
- Rotate the hips
- Level swing

< As your body starts to rotate, your top hand should be pulling the bat through the strike zone.

The swing also involves rotating on the ball of your back foot. >

The Mechanics of the Swing

Special Situations

1 When facing a very fast pitcher, you may want to place your stance farther back in the batter's box to give you more reaction time. You may also want to start your load and stride a little earlier then usual.

2 For a slower pitcher, or one that throws a lot of off-speed pitches, you may want to move your stance up in the batter's box. Slow or off-speed pitches tend to drop below the hitters knees as they reach the catcher.

3 Hitting the Curve involves, first of all, recognizing that it is a curve. Study the pitcher when he warms up and when he faces other batters to see if he has a curve and if so, does he throw it any differently than his fastball (lower arm slot, cocked wrist, etc.) The curve ball has a different spin than a fastball so the earlier you pick up the spin of the ball the better. If you keep your hands and weight back properly you should still be in a good position to hit the curve. Also, quite often at the younger age, it is very difficult for the younger pitcher to throw the curve for a strike, so you may want to lay off of it until you fall behind in the count.

4 With two strikes, you may need to make some adjustments. Move a little closer to the plate and widen your stance just a little. Choke-up on the bat. This will help you shorten your swing and get better control.

< The Stance
Feet should be a little more than shoulder width apart and weight equally balanced. Hips and shoulders should be parallel to the ground and knees bent slightly.

The Load >
Shift your weight toward the back foot and keep your upper body coiled and ready to spring. Bat should be held about shoulder high and back toward the catcher.

< The Stride
Take a short, soft, stride toward the pitcher, but keep your hands and weight back.

The Swing >
The knob of the bat should move toward the ball. Rotate on your back foot (squashing the bug). Keep your head steady. Your body stays over the hips—don't lunge. Focus on the ball and make contact.

Mike Sandlock

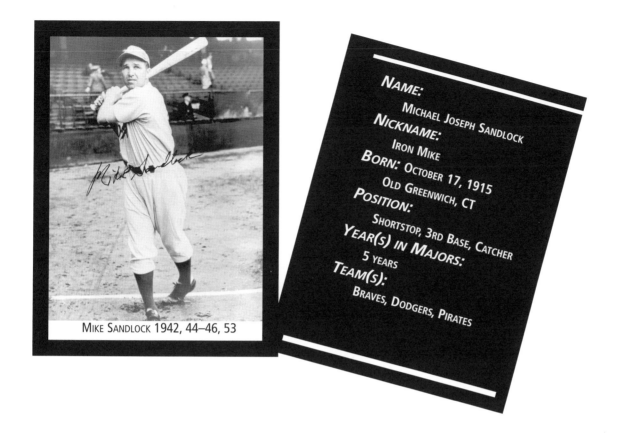

MIKE SANDLOCK 1942, 44–46, 53

NAME: MICHAEL JOSEPH SANDLOCK

NICKNAME: IRON MIKE

BORN: OCTOBER 17, 1915 OLD GREENWICH, CT

POSITION: SHORTSTOP, 3RD BASE, CATCHER

YEAR(S) IN MAJORS: 5 YEARS

TEAM(S): BRAVES, DODGERS, PIRATES

As a rookie with the Boston Braves in 1942, Sandlock was paid exactly $75 a month for his services. A versatile and talented player, he had the ability to play all the infield positions and was primarily a catcher for the Brooklyn Dodgers during the 1945 and 1946 seasons. His best year came in 1945 with the Dodgers. Appearing in 80 games, he racked up 55 hits, 14 doubles and 2 home runs for a .282 batting average. After the 1946 season, Sandlock played Triple A ball with Montreal in the International League and with Hollywood in the Pacific Coast League for 6 years. The ability to handle the difficult knuckle ball brought him back to the majors in 1953 with the Pirates. Mike was inducted into the Brooklyn Dodger Hall of Fame in 1998.

Jim, if your son is interested in baseball, that's fine. You must work at all the things that you're not very good at. Work and work! The one thing I neglected was my school work. Many years ago it wasn't so important. Today, if you do not have a degree it's going to be tough on you. Don't worry too much about baseball, scouts are at all the schools.

Jim Delsing

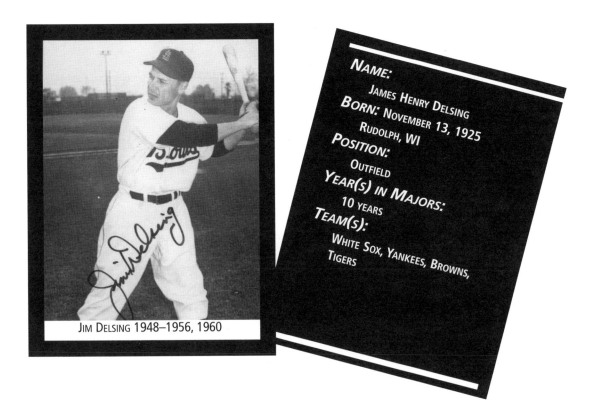

JIM DELSING 1948–1956, 1960

NAME:
JAMES HENRY DELSING
BORN: NOVEMBER 13, 1925
RUDOLPH, WI
POSITION:
OUTFIELD
YEAR(S) IN MAJORS:
10 YEARS
TEAM(S):
WHITE SOX, YANKEES, BROWNS, TIGERS

Jim Delsing began his career with the White Sox in 1948. A left-handed line-drive hitter with a good eye, he usually walked more than he struck out. His best year was with the 1953 Detroit Tigers, with 11 home runs, 62 RBIs and a .288 batting average. He was a steady and reliable fielder who hit .300 several times in the minors and made the Northern League, Pacific Coast League, and American Association all-star teams on his way to the majors. He was with the Yankees for the 1949 season, a team that went on to beat the Brooklyn Dodgers in the World Series. After retiring from baseball, Delsing became an advertising salesman for the St. Louis Review. His son Jay is a member of the PGA tour.

" For Nicholas, my advice is play, play, play, and practice his skills. Learn your weak points, correct them, and just practice and improve all the parts of your game. Become a full player, being able to be a good runner, fielder, hitter, and a good thinker. My Best Wishes. "

Jim Delsing

On August 18, 1951, at Sportsman's Park in St. Louis, Jim Delsing was part of the most publicized stunt in baseball history. Bill Veeck, owner of the St. Louis Browns, saw baseball as entertainment, and his clubs always had a carnival-like element. He staged morning games during World War II for workers coming off the graveyard shift, let fans decide the game strategy with voting cards, sold mirrors to fans in the bleachers to shine in enemy batters' eyes, and rigged the fences so that they could be moved in and out to his teams advantage.

On August 18, to the surprise of the fans, 3' 7" 65 lb midget Eddie Gaedel emerged from a seven-foot birthday cake between games of a Tigers doubleheader. The cake was to celebrate the 50th anniversary of the American League. Gaedel, a stage performer, was wearing a Browns uniform with the number 1/8, and little slippers that looked like elf's shoes. In the bottom of the first inning, the Browns manager sent Gaedel in to pinch hit for the lead off batter. Veeck had secretly signed Gaedel to a contract several days before. Over the objections of Detroit Manager Red Rolfe, the umpire allowed Gaedel to bat.

In his stance, Gaedel's strike zone measured 1-1/2 inches. Detroit pitcher Bob Cain walked the midget, throwing four straight balls. Once at first base, Delsing was sent in to pinch run and the crowd gave Gaedel a standing ovation. American League president William Harridge was furious over the incident and unsuccessfully tried to strike Gaedel's name from the record books.

Jim Delsing had his name placed in baseball history that day. Says Delsing, "As long as they remember you. A lot of people say Maris hit 61, but I'm the only one who ran for a midget."

Johnny Hopp

JOHNNY HOPP 1939–1952

NAME:
John Leonard Hopp
NICKNAME:
Hippity
BORN: July 18, 1916
Hastings, NE
POSITION:
1st Base, Outfield
YEAR(S) IN MAJORS:
14 years
TEAM(S):
Cardinals, Braves, Dodgers,
Pirates, Yankees, Tigers
CAREER HIGHLIGHTS:
All-Star in 1946

John Hopp was a player with great enthusiasm for the game of baseball. At age 19, he was signed by a Yankee farm team in Norfolk, Nebraska. In 1939 he was picked up by the St. Louis Cardinals and quickly became part of the crazy and daring "Gas House Gang." 1941 was Johnny's first season as a regular, when he filled in for the injured Johnny Mize at first base for the Cards. He was so successful that St. Louis traded Mize to the Giants. Hopp went on to play 7 seasons with the Cardinals, leading them to three National League Championships and two World Series Championships. After 7 years with the Cardinals he was traded to the Braves and wasted no

time establishing himself as the team's leading hitter. After several short stops with the Pirates and Dodgers, he was traded to the Yankees in 1950, where he won two more World Series rings. Besides being an all-star in 1946 with the Cardinals, between 1941 and 1949 Johnny was in the top ten in stolen bases 8 times, in triples 6 times, and in batting average twice. His career ended abruptly in 1952, when he injured his hamstring while playing for the Detroit Tigers, an injury he would never recover from. He finished his career coaching before he retired.

" *Develop discipline in all that you do.* "

Letter from Johnny Hopp

"

Jim,

The best advice I can offer is run, run, run. Every athlete needs good legs and running speed does help. I used to run to grade school 1 mile, ran home for lunch, and then ran back to school. We ran races in my neighborhood. Soon I became very fast in high school, college and pro ball. Swing a bat when you have idle time, lift bar bells and develop your strength in hands, forearms, and shoulders. Play catch with a buddy. Develop control. Never throw too hard over a long period of time. Stay away from throwing a curve ball, save your arm. No smoking, ever!! Develop discipline in all that you do. Be good to your body and it will be good to you. I'll be 81 on July 18th, I still eat good foods and I feel great. Tell your boy to have fun in sports.

"

Johnny Hopp

Don Gutteridge

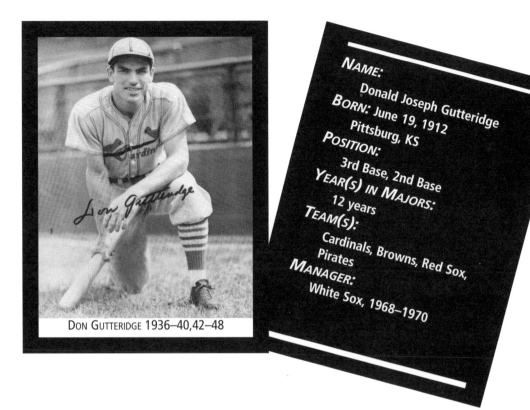

DON GUTTERIDGE 1936–40,42–48

NAME:
Donald Joseph Gutteridge
BORN: June 19, 1912
Pittsburg, KS
POSITION:
3rd Base, 2nd Base
YEAR(S) IN MAJORS:
12 years
TEAM(S):
Cardinals, Browns, Red Sox, Pirates
MANAGER:
White Sox, 1968–1970

Don Gutteridge can truly boast, that he has dedicated his life to the game of baseball. As a player, scout, manager, or coach, he spent over fifty years in the game. The high point of his career came on his second day in a Cardinal uniform. In a double-header against the Brooklyn Dodgers, the rookie got 6 hits, including an inside-the-park home run, and stole home plate twice. Don is one of only 70 players to play for both the St. Louis Cardinals and the St. Louis Browns. Known as a sharp, sure-footed second baseman, he helped lead the Browns to the World Series in 1944 and was with the Boston Red Sox in 1946, when they lost the World Series to the Cardinals in seven games. Gutteridge was a coach for the 1959 White Sox World Series team and was a coach for the 1955, 1960, 1961, and 1966 All Star teams. Don also authored the book *Don Gutteridge In Words And Pictures*, which features great stories from his baseball playing days. His cousin, Ray Mueller, played for the Boston Braves and the Pittsburgh Pirates.

My advice is to practice, practice, practice. But practice correctly. Get good advice from a good teacher and never practice doing things the wrong way, even if it seems like it is the right thing.

Johnny Blanchard

JOHNNY BLANCHARD 1955, 59–65

NAME:
John Edwin Blanchard
BORN: February 26, 1933
Minneapolis, MN
POSITION:
Outfield, Catcher
YEAR(S) IN MAJORS:
8 years
TEAM(S):
Yankees, Athletics, Braves

Johnny Blanchard savored his position as the Yankees' third-string catcher for most of his career. He was a backup for Yogi Berra and Elston Howard. When given the chance, Blanchard responded in 1961 with adequate defense and a career-best .305, 21 HR season. Johnny appeared in 5 straight World Series with the Yankees (1960–1964) and holds the record with ten World Series pinch-hitting appearances. The 1961 New York Yankees were one of the most successful teams in baseball history. This was the year when Mickey Mantle and Roger Maris battled it out for the home run crown. What may have been lost was the effort put together by other members of the team. Bill Skowron, Yogi Berra, Johnny Blanchard, and Elston Howard each had more than 20 home runs. As a team, the Yankees led the American League with 240 home runs that year. He once hit home runs in 4 consecutive at-bats.

> **Nick, You must play baseball every day, all summer. If you are a catcher, practice throwing the ball to second base from home plate. Just playing catch will strengthen your arm. You don't have to throw hard. Just lob the ball that distance (to begin). If you can learn to throw runners out, you will be in the Big Leagues.**

Alvin Dark

ALVIN DARK 1946, 1948–1960

NAME: Alvin Ralph Dark
NICKNAME: The Swamp Fox
BORN: January 7, 1922 Comanche, OK
POSITION: Shortstop, 3rd Base, 2nd Base
YEAR(S) IN MAJORS: 14 years
TEAM(S): Braves, Giants, Cardinals, Cubs, Phillies
CAREER HIGHLIGHTS: Rookie of the year in 1948

Dark, a 3-time all-star, earned Rookie of the Year honors with the Boston Braves in 1948. A talented athlete in both high school and college, he went on to become a consistent and dangerous hitter in the Major Leagues. Between 1948 and 1958, Dark was in the top ten in batting average 3 times, hits 7 times, doubles 5 times, triples 3 times. During that same time period, he led the league in games played 5 times, at-bats 7 times, and hit .300 four times. Al appeared in three World Series contests, once with the Boston Braves (1948) and twice with the New York Giants (1951 and 1954). His single in the ninth inning of he 1951 National League playoff game started the rally that ended in Bobby Thomson's famous pennant-winning homer. In 1954 he helped lead the Giants to a World Series victory. He finished up his playing career in 1960, splitting the season between the Phillies and the Braves. He managed the San Francisco Giants in 1961 and guided the Giants to the National League pennant the next year. After managing in Cleveland for 4 years, he took the 1974 and 1975 Oakland A's to the American League pennant and to a World Series victory in 1974

My priorities had been baseball, baseball, baseball, and then golf and more golf. I knew that I needed to set new priorities which put God first in my life.

Letter from Alvin Dark

"Dear Jim and Nick,

During my earlier days in baseball, if anyone had told me that one day I would exchange a bat and the dugout for a Bible, golf clubs and attendance at a women's Bible class, I would have laughed it off as the joke of the year. Yet beginning in 1971, when taking time off from baseball, all this came to pass. Everybody in baseball knows that firing is part of the game, but it's not something you get used to. At that same time, I was struggling with some deep family problems too. Underneath I was hurting, and plagued with bouts of depression.

Golf came first and I decided to submerge myself in the game. I played so much that I began to neglect my wife and our children, but it seemed that I couldn't help myself. Secretly, I was glad when my wife, Jackie, began to attend a Bible class at our church. Each week she came home excited about what she was learning. I began to notice a change in her outlook and a perking up of her spirits. This continued until one morning when I said, "Wait for me. I'm going too." I began reading and studying the Bible each week with my wife. It was like searching for buried treasure. As part of my Bible studies I learned to relate to some of the men of God in the Bible. Abraham, Job, Moses, Peter and others—they'd all had periods of disobedience, but that didn't stop God from loving them or using them again, once they had repented. Those men gradually became more real in my life and offered important examples on how nothing in life is right if your priorities are mixed up. My priorities had been baseball, baseball, baseball, and then golf and more golf. I knew that I needed to set new priorities which put God first in my life.

When I got back into baseball in 1974, first as manager of the Oakland Athletics, as a coach for the Cubs, and manager for the Padres, my faith was tested over and over. It wasn't easy standing up for what I believed. Do I miss baseball? Baseball has been my business for 30 years and I believe I know it well. But it is not my life. Jesus Christ is the center of that. I would urge any youngster or ballplayer to accept Jesus Christ as their personal savior and make their walk with God a priority."

Your Friend, Al Dark

Mace Brown

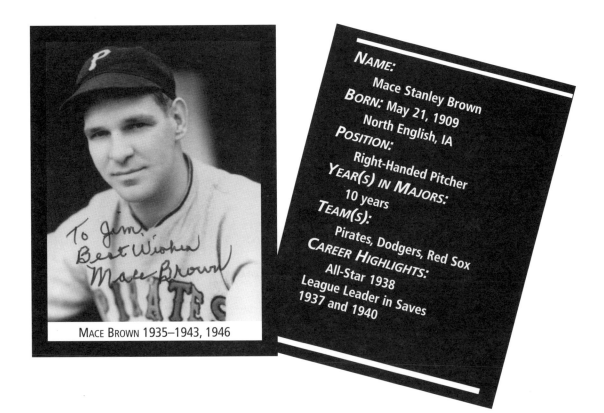

MACE BROWN 1935–1943, 1946

NAME:
Mace Stanley Brown
BORN: May 21, 1909
North English, IA
POSITION:
Right-Handed Pitcher
YEAR(S) IN MAJORS:
10 years
TEAM(S):
Pirates, Dodgers, Red Sox
CAREER HIGHLIGHTS:
All-Star 1938
League Leader in Saves
1937 and 1940

Mace Brown was originally signed by the St. Louis Cardinals in 1930, but it was with Pittsburgh, Brooklyn and Boston that he would contribute during his 10 year career. As a rookie with the Pirates, Brown was present on May 25, 1935 when Babe Ruth hit his last three home runs. After Ruth hit his third home run he headed for the showers and had to pass through the Pirate's dugout to get there. Ruth sat down on the bench right next to Mace and said, "Boys, that last one felt good." Brown's best season came in 1938 when he posted a 15–9 record, appearing in a league-leading 51 games and was selected for the All Star team. One of the first relief specialists, he set a record in 1937 by making 50 appearances without recording a complete game. After his playing days, Mace Brown worked as a scout and instructor for the Red Sox from 1947 until he retired at the age of 80 in 1990. He also served in the Navy from 1944 to 1945.

" My advice to your son is to play all he can. Play a lot of catch, throw a lot to strengthen your arm and hit a lot. "

Chapter 2

The Mental Aspects of Hitting

Rick Wise
Boston Red Sox

Al Pilarcik
Kansas City Athletics

Billy Hitchcock
Philadelphia Athletics

Johnny Lucadello
St. Louis Cardinals

Jerry Kindall
Team USA

Pete Coscarart
Brooklyn Dodgers

Al Worthington
Minnesota Twins

Sam Chapman
Philadelphia Athletics

The Mental Aspects of Hitting

Mental Aspects

1 Chances are, by the age of 10, you have had a lot of instruction in the mechanics of hitting. Most of this instruction has come from parents and coaches who have a genuine interest in helping you to improve.

2 Another part of hitting is the mental aspect. The batter who is mentally prepared can have a great advantage, not only over the pitcher, but the other team as well. This is not always easy, but if you take the time to be mentally prepared you'll become a better ballplayer.

3 It takes work and patience, but this is where good ballplayers are made.

4 The mental aspects of hitting involve:

- Knowing the other team
- Having a strategy
- Knowing the pitcher
- Knowing the umpire
- Working the count

5 We will look at each of these aspects briefly, and give you some tips on how they may all work together to your advantage.

Knowing The Other Team

1 Have you looked over at the other team, just before a game, to see which pitcher is warming up and how the team is doing during their infield warm ups? Have you ever "sized up" the other team to determine what your chances are of winning?

2 This is part of getting to know the other team. If you watch the other team closely, you'll see that they have certain ways of doing things. A good hitter will watch and study the opposing team to find out what their strong and weak points are.

3 Before a game, watch the coach as the team warms up. Is a player in left field because of a strong arm or his weak arm? Who takes the cut off throws on a ball hit to the outfield? Pre-game warm-ups is the best time to evaluate some of the individual players on the other team. The coach will have his/her own philosophy of playing and the whole team will reflect this philosophy. Watch how the opposing coach directs the players.

4 Watch the team during the course of the game. Are there certain situations when they try a pick-off move? Evaluate the strengths and weaknesses of the catcher. Does he have a quick, accurate throw to second base? If the catcher is calling the pitches, is the first pitch to every batter a fastball?

5 Some coaches, at the 12 and over level, call the pitches instead of letting the catcher do it. A coach is going to call for certain pitches in certain situations. Maybe he likes seeing a breaking ball on every 2–2 count. If the coach insists on calling the pitches, he will probably have a routine and stick to it. If you can figure out his routine, it doesn't matter which of his pitchers is on the mound, the pitch selection will always be the same. If you're not sure if the coach or the catcher is calling the pitches, watch the catcher between pitches. If he looks over to the dugout before every pitch, the coach is probably giving the signs.

The Mental Aspects of Hitting

Having a Strategy

1 Each time good hitters approach the plate they have an idea of what they want to do. When you're younger, you just want to have a good swing, make contact with the ball, and get a hit. As you get older it takes a lot more thought.

2 Good hitters need to decide for themselves, before they step into the batter's box, what they want to accomplish. If you're leading off at the beginning of the game or an inning, the proper thing to do might be to go as deep in the count as possible. This makes the pitcher throw as many pitches as possible and give your teammates a good chance to see how the pitcher is throwing.

3 Being impatient or careless could cause a quick out, giving the other team and the pitcher, an advantage. If it's late in the game and your team really needs base runners, your plan might be to get on base anyway you can. This may mean getting a walk if you have to.

4 If there is a runner on second base and no one out, a good hitter is going to try to hit the ball to the right side of the field. That way, a ground ball to the second baseman moves the runner to third base where he can score on a sacrifice fly. That same grounder, if hit to the shortstop, forces the runner to stay at second base and you've given up an out without getting anything in return.

5 Each time you go into the batter's box you should be thinking about what you can do to help your team win.

6 Your strategy can change, even within the same at bat. If you go up to bat with one out and a runner on second, you might start off thinking that you want a hit to drive in the run. But, if the pitcher gets two strikes on you, suddenly your strategy is changed. Now, you just want to protect the plate and not strike out. A hit, a walk, or a ground ball to the right side of the field might move the runner to third and let the next batter have a chance to drive in the run. You started the at-bat with an aggressive strategy, and ended it with a defensive strategy. The point is, you had an idea of what you wanted to do the entire time.

7 Keep in mind that there are times when your coach will determine your strategy. This may not be easy for the player who wants to swing-away and the coach gives the signal to bunt or to take a pitch. Remember to follow the instructions of your Coach, he will determine what is best for the team.

Remember:

- Have a strategy each time you approach the plate.

- Think about what you need to accomplish.

- Think about what is needed to help your team win.

The Mental Aspects of Hitting

Knowing The Pitcher

1 Good hitters should try to learn everything they can about the pitcher. If you have had to face him/her before, you might know something about the opposing pitcher. If you haven't seen the pitcher before, you can still pick up on things by watching them closely during the game, starting with warm ups before the game even starts.

2 By understanding the game situation and the pitcher, you will be able to make an educated guess about the type of pitch he is going to throw you.

3 Watch the pitcher closely before the game as he throws his warm up pitches. How much power and control does he have? Is he making a good effort to warm up properly or is he just playing around? Is he throwing a breaking ball or a knuckleball and is he getting it over for strikes? Note whether the pitcher is a left-hander or right-hander. If the pitcher is throwing from the same side as you (righty vs. righty or lefty vs. lefty) then you need to remember that a breaking ball is going to be moving away from you as it crosses the plate, and the fastball will also have a slight angle away from you. When you face the pitcher from the opposite side (lefty vs. righty or righty vs. lefty) the opposite is true.

4 When the game begins watch everything that the pitcher does. You can observe what kind of breaking ball he throws and how well it's breaking. You'll also see how he pitches to other batters. Does he throw a fastball as his first pitch every time or does he mix it up?

5 Many pitchers will throw the same pitch when they are either ahead in the count or behind in the count. Is he struggling with his control or is he hitting the corners of the strike zone with his fastball? The ability to make these observations and to learn from them is the sign of a good hitter.

6 Pay particular attention to the pitcher's motion when he throws his different pitches. Sometimes a pitcher will give himself away. For example, when he throws a curve ball, his arm comes right over the top of his head but, when he throws a fastball, his arm drops a little. Keep an eye on his windup. Is it quick or does he take his time? Knowing something like this will help you time the pitches when you're up at bat.

7 Sometimes, after getting the sign from the catcher, the pitcher will go right into the windup if it's a fast ball. If it's a breaking ball, he might take a second or two to adjust his grip after getting the sign. Most hitters will not pick up on little clues like this, but it is often the difference between getting a hit and striking out. Pay attention to how he pitches to you, especially if you strike out. If he gets you to swing at a high fastball for strike three, the next time you're up and have two strikes, that's probably the pitch you will see. If a pitcher is successful in the way he pitches to you this time, it's probably the way he's going to pitch to you the next time.

8 Finally, keep an eye on the pitcher when someone's on base. If you watch a pitcher closely enough, you can get to know his pick-off move. Most pitchers will give little clues without even knowing it. Sometimes a pitcher will stand on the rubber a little differently, or hold his glove back toward second base so that he can shorten up his throw to first base. If you can identify these small details, it will give you an advantage as a base runner, as well as a batter.

The Mental Aspects of Hitting

Remember:

- Learn as much as you can about the pitcher before and during the game.
- What type of pitches does he throw and when does he throw them?
- Study the pitcher's motion and form.
- Look for clues that can help give you an advantage.

Knowing The Umpire

1 Up to this point, you've been taught to go up to the plate, wait for a good pitch, and swing the bat. Now that you are older, the umpires are going to be much stricter with the strike zone that they call.

2 A good hitter must learn to be patient. Don't help out the umpire and the pitcher by swinging at bad pitches. You must remember that the umpire is getting a totally different view of the ball and the plate than you are. You can follow the ball with your eyes until it's a few feet in front of the plate; after that, you cannot really see it. The umpire can see the ball come across the plate, as well as its final resting place.

3 If you think that the umpire is not calling a certain pitch the way it should be called, there are ways that you can try to influence him to get the calls in your favor. When doing this, it's important not to be angry or to accuse the umpire of making a mistake.

4 When you have an opportunity, approach the umpire and politely ask about the pitcher's breaking ball, or those high inside strikes. Tell the umpire that you're just trying to get a better understanding of his calls.

5 It is acceptable to tell the umpire that you thought that the pitch was a little high, or a little low. Comments or questions, as long as they are polite and in a conversational tone, are acceptable and a good hitter might even gain an advantage by having the umpire describe how these pitches are strikes.

6 It is acceptable to approach the umpire, even before the game has started, to ask him what his strike zone is. This is a legitimate question, and most umpires are pleased to give out this information.

7 The umpire will not adjust his calls to where you think the strike zone should be. A smart hitter will watch the umpire and determine what the umpire's zone is, and then adjust.

Remember:

- Ask the umpire before the game where his strike zone is.
- A player may politely ask about a questionable pitch.
- A player may not argue balls and strikes.
- Remember that the umpire is always right, even when he is wrong.

The Mental Aspects of Hitting

Working The Count

1 Have you ever swung wildly at a pitch you thought was a fastball, only to learn that the pitcher threw an off-speed pitch? Sometimes a pitcher may fool you, and from time to time you may swing at a bad pitch. What will help you the most as a hitter is to have an idea of what kind of pitch to expect. The key to understanding what type of pitch is coming is to know the pitch-count situation.

2 There are basically four different situations:

- The 0–0 count
- The 3–2 count
- The pitcher's count
- The hitter's count

The 0–0 Count

1 It is difficult to guess what's coming on the first pitch, but this can be a very important count. If you have been watching the pitcher, either in the current game or in previous games you might actually have an idea of what type of pitches he throws.

2 Most pitchers, in the 12 and older leagues, rely heavily on the fastball. The fastball is the pitch they have thrown the most and feel most confident in. It is the pitch most often thrown on a 0–0 count.

3 During your time at bat, most pitchers will also try to mix things up in order to keep you guessing. It's important that you don't make an out on the first pitch. Not swinging until you get the first strike is not a bad strategy. If the first pitch is an easy fastball right down the middle, you are going to want to take a crack at it while you have the chance.

But, if you ground out on a breaking ball outside of the strike zone, you've given the pitcher one out on one pitch.

4 The general rule is: For your first pitch look for a fastball in the heart of the strike zone, and if you get one, go for it; otherwise, let that pitch go and work from there.

The 3–2 Count

1 This is the most interesting count because it puts equal pressure on both the hitter and the pitcher. You don't want a strike out, and the pitcher does not want you on base. Except for a foul ball, something is going to happen on this pitch.

2 One thing to consider is what your at-bat means to the pitcher. If the count is 3–2 in the bottom of the last inning, with the score tied and the bases loaded, you'll probably see his best pitch.

3 For the batter, a full count does not necessarily have to be a pressure situation. A 3–2 count on the first batter in the first inning is not a big deal.

4 The most important thing for the batter to do is to stay as calm and as relaxed as possible. Make sure that you protect the plate. This means that you should swing at any pitch within the strike zone, and at any pitch which is even near the strike zone. Keep in mind that during the early innings and when a pitcher does not feel threatened, he may rely on a curve ball or off speed pitch on the 3–2 count.

5 The general rule is: Swing at any pitch which is near the strike zone and protect the plate.

The Mental Aspects of Hitting

The Pitcher's Count

1 The pitcher's count includes the 0–1, 0–2, and the 1–2 counts. This means that the pitcher has pitches to waste, but the hitter does not. Even 2–2 is a pitcher's count, especially if he started out behind in the count and came back to even it up.

2 The rules here are the same as in the 3–2 count; the only difference is that there's not really any pressure on the pitcher and he can throw any pitch he wants without worrying about a walk.

3 This is where you should look for his best secondary pitch. If the pitcher throws a good curve or slider, that's what you'll see. This is the time that the pitcher wants to fool you and make you think you're seeing a fastball, only to swing at an off speed, or back away from a curve ball across the plate.

4 The general rule is: On this count, you will not see a fastball down the heart of the plate. The pitcher will try to fool you with a secondary pitch or try to get you to swing at a ball outside of the strike zone. If the pitch is close, protect the plate.

The Hitter's Count

1 The hitter's count includes the 2–0, 3–0, 2–1, and the 3–1 count. These counts give the advantage to the hitter because pitchers do not like to fall behind and don't like to see walks. The hitter now has pitches to waste, but the pitcher does not.

2 If the pitcher gets behind in the count, he's going to throw something he's pretty sure he can get a strike with. The hitter should expect a fastball.

3 The most common pitch in a 3–0 count is a fastball down the heart of the plate. This is true for several reasons. First, the pitcher wants to be sure of a strike. He also counts on the possibility that the hitter may foul off the pitch, or even better, hit a weak ground-ball for an out. The pitcher also knows that most coaches give the "take sign" to most batters with this count. If the coach tells you to take the pitch, you should take the pitch. If the coach gives you the green light make sure that the fast ball is in your hitting zone.

4 The general rule is: The hitter should expect a fastball.

Rick Wise

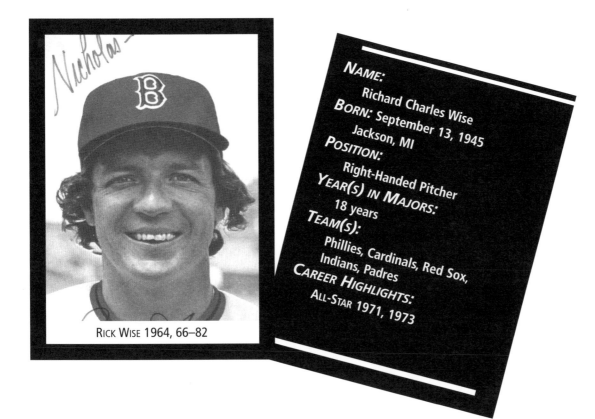

RICK WISE 1964, 66–82

NAME:
Richard Charles Wise
BORN: September 13, 1945
Jackson, MI
POSITION:
Right-Handed Pitcher
YEAR(S) IN MAJORS:
18 years
TEAM(S):
Phillies, Cardinals, Red Sox,
Indians, Padres
CAREER HIGHLIGHTS:
ALL-STAR 1971, 1973

Rick Wise was a star high-school athlete in Portland, Oregon. He signed a bonus contract with Philadelphia in 1963, and went 5–3 as an 18-year-old for the 1964 Phillies. The hard thrower was sent down to the minor leagues in 1965, but returned in 1966 and had mixed success for several years. In 1971 he went 17–14 and no-hit Cincinnati on June 23, becoming the only pitcher in Major League history to hit two home runs in a no-hitter. He was considered one of the best-hitting pitchers in the National League with a .195 career average and 15 home runs. In the spring of 1972 he was traded to the Cardinals for pitcher Steve Carlton. Rick won 16 games for St. Louis in both 1972 and 1973 and was the winning pitcher in the 1973 All-Star game. In 1974 he was traded to the Red Sox and won 19 games in 1975 to help Boston to the American League Championship. He was the winning pitcher, in relief, in the sixth game of the World Series that year, won by Carlton Fisk's dramatic home run. He is currently the pitching coach for the Nashua Pride of the Atlantic League.

" Jim, The hand-eye coordination necessary to hit a baseball, for average or power, takes many, many hours of practice. Go to the baseball diamonds and batting cages as often as possible. Be a good listener to your coaches or instructors and be willing to dedicate yourself to being the best baseball player you can be. Above all, enjoy the great game of baseball and watch it or play it as often as possible. "

Al Pilarcik

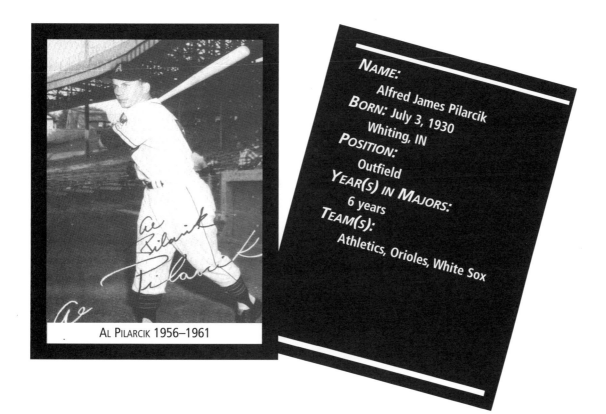

AL PILARCIK 1956–1961

NAME:
Alfred James Pilarcik
BORN: July 3, 1930
Whiting, IN
POSITION:
Outfield
YEAR(S) IN MAJORS:
6 years
TEAM(S):
Athletics, Orioles, White Sox

Al Pilarcik began his professional baseball career joining the Yankees' farm system in 1948 at Independence, Kansas where he batted .299. A smooth fielder, he proceeded to climb every rung of the baseball ladder from class "D" to "AAA" in just seven seasons. In 1956, his rookie year with the Kansas City Athletics, he appeared in only 69 games but had 60 hits, 22 RBIs and 9 stolen bases. After being traded to the Orioles in 1957, Al became a regular outfielder, playing all three outfield positions. His best season came with the Orioles in 1957 when he hit .278 with nine homers and finished second in the American League in outfield assists. After retiring from baseball, he spent twenty seasons as a high school varsity coach.

> *This may sound odd, but a person should be respectful of others. Some players are good with their skills but cancerous to a team because as a person, they are rotten on the inside. Just be a good person!*

Billy Hitchcock

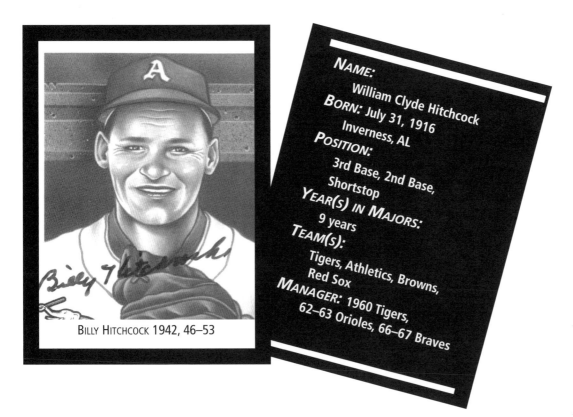

BILLY HITCHCOCK 1942, 46–53

NAME: William Clyde Hitchcock
BORN: July 31, 1916 Inverness, AL
POSITION: 3rd Base, 2nd Base, Shortstop
YEAR(S) IN MAJORS: 9 years
TEAM(S): Tigers, Athletics, Browns, Red Sox
MANAGER: 1960 Tigers, 62–63 Orioles, 66–67 Braves

Billy Hitchcock attended Auburn University and excelled at both football and baseball. Originally drafted by the Yankees in 1938, he spent 1943 through 1945 in Army Air Force where he received the Bronze Medal for his service in the Pacific. He was a versatile player that could play all four infield positions. His best year came in 1950 with the Athletics when he hit .273 and had 22 doubles. He played baseball until 1953, but his association with baseball would not end for another 27 years. Hitchcock went on to coach and scout and then become the manager of the Baltimore Orioles for the 1962 and 1963 seasons and the Atlanta Braves during the 1966 and 1967 seasons. In 1971 Billy became the president of the Southern league and stayed until his retirement in 1980.

Dear Jim, My advice to a 14-year-old is very simple. Eat properly, drink the right drinks, don't smoke, don't do drugs, keep yourself in shape physically, practice hard, play hard, always give it 100% (Your very best), listen to your coaches, be receptive to coaching, be confident but not cocky, and believe that you can do the job. Good luck Nicholas—I hope to get to see you playing for the Boston Red Sox in about 10 years. Practice hard—Play Hard!

Johnny Lucadello

JOHNNY LUCADELLO 1938–41, 46–47

NAME:
John Lucadello
BORN: February 22, 1919
Thurber, TX
POSITION:
2nd Base, 3rd Base
YEAR(S) IN MAJORS:
6 years
TEAM(S):
Browns, Yankees

During the summer of 1936, 16-year-old Johnny Lucadello found himself racing around the bases for the Fostoria Red Birds of the Ohio State League. He had been visiting his brother, Tony, who was playing shortstop for the Red Birds. The regular second baseman was forced out of the lineup due to an injury and Tony suggested that his kid brother fill in. Johnny was signed and played for 3 weeks. During 1937 and 1938, he played in the Nebraska State League and the Mid-Atlantic League. He batted over .300 and made the all-star team both seasons. In 1938, he was called up to finish the American League season with the St. Louis Browns. During his playing years, Lucadello bounced between the majors and minors. He served in the Navy from 1942 to 1945. On September 16, 1940 Lucadello hit home runs from each side of the plate. Prior to Lucadello, Wally Schang had been the last American League player to accomplish the feat. It would not happen again until Mickey Mantle did it in 1955. After his playing career, John scouted for the Cubs, White Sox and Phillies.

> *Dear Jim, I have received your request for my husband's autograph for your baseball collection. Unfortunately, my husband has recently passed away (10-30-01). He would want you to have this autographed photo of him in his rookie year with the St. Louis Browns in 1941. Please tell your son that John would want him to believe in himself and to follow his dreams. Sincerely Yours, Mrs. John Lucadello*

Jerry Kindall

JERRY KINDALL 1556–58, 60–65

NAME:
Gerald Donald Kindall
NICKNAME:
Slim
BORN: May 27, 1935
St. Paul, MN
POSITION:
Shortstop, 2nd Base, 1st Base
YEAR(S) IN MAJORS:
9 years
TEAM(S):
Cubs, Indians, Twins

A native of St. Paul Minnesota, Jerry Kindall played both basketball and baseball at the University of Minnesota. In 1956 he was All-American shortstop as Minnesota beat Arizona in the College World Series. In July 1956, Kindall signed a bonus contract with the Chicago Cubs. He played 9 years as an infielder with three different teams including the 1965 American League Champion Minnesota Twins. Perhaps his greatest accomplishments were during his 24 years as head baseball coach for the University of Arizona. During that time he led Arizona to three NCAA Championships, three PAC 6 Championships, and was College Baseball "Coach of the Year" three times. Jerry also coached the 1979, 1991 and 1999 USA baseball teams. In addition to playing and coaching. Kindall has authored several baseball books including: *The Science of Coaching Baseball* and *The Baseball Coaching Bible*.

" *Hi Nicholas, Take every opportunity to practice and play baseball. Skip the video games, MTV, and TV and look for friends who like to play baseball. Also, it is a sign of inner strength and courage to say "NO" to alcohol, tobacco, drugs, as well as vulgar, profane language. College and professional scouts are looking for good players who do, say, and believe the right things. God Bless you.* "

Pete Coscarart

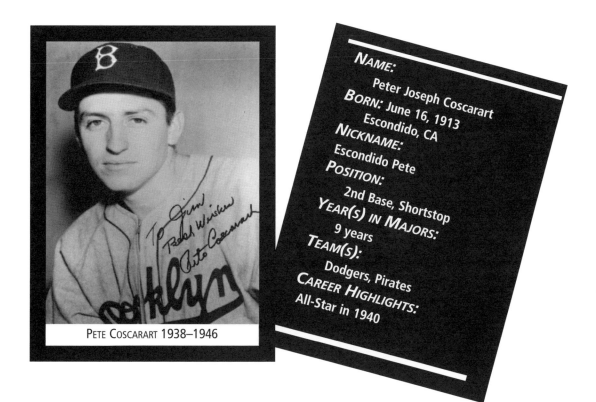

PETE COSCARART 1938–1946

NAME:
Peter Joseph Coscarart
BORN: June 16, 1913
Escondido, CA
NICKNAME:
Escondido Pete
POSITION:
2nd Base, Shortstop
YEAR(S) IN MAJORS:
9 years
TEAM(S):
Dodgers, Pirates
CAREER HIGHLIGHTS:
All-Star in 1940

Pete Coscarart along with his brothers, Joe and Steve, all played baseball in Portland, OR, and all three had a dream of making it to the big leagues together. Pete and Joe did, but their brother Steve was injured before his dream was realized. Pete mainly played second base during his career and in 1940 was selected for the All-Star team. In 1941 he was part of the Dodger team that played New York in the World Series. Following his baseball career, Pete worked as a scout for the Minnesota Twins and the New York Yankees. He worked in real estate for 30 years after his baseball days.

Dear Jim, It was nice to hear from a great fan. I receive many letters from the New York area for my autograph—I never turn anyone down. With the way salaries are today, I guess I was born too soon! My advice to your 14-year-old son is to never give up. Play as much as you can, no matter where, keep playing. When I was 14 years old I weighed 90 pounds. Just a shrimp. But I loved to play baseball and I kept playing and playing! I certainly want to wish you luck in your profession. I think that it is a dangerous job these days. That's the way I feel about all policemen. You guys are my heroes. May God protect you always. I am enclosing a couple of baseball cards for Nick. Best Regards.

Al Worthington

AL WORTHINGTON 53–54,56–60,63–69

NAME:
Allan Fulton Worthington
NICKNAME:
Red
BORN: February 5, 1929
Birmingham, AL
POSITION:
Right-Handed Pitcher
YEAR(S) IN MAJORS:
14 years
TEAM(S):
Giants, Red Sox, White Sox,
Reds, Twins
CAREER HIGHLIGHTS:
League Leader in Saves: 1968

Worthington, up to the big leagues in 1953 with the NY Giants, threw shutouts in his first 2 games. In 1958, his best year, he won 11 games mostly coming out of the bullpen. During the 1959 season, he had heard that the Giants had placed a spy in the outfield bleachers. The spy, using binoculars, could see the signs from the visiting team's catcher and then alert the batter as to what pitch was coming. Worthington told his manager that he believed that sign stealing was cheating and that if it didn't stop, that he would have to leave the team. Shortly after, Al was traded to the Boston Red Sox. After a short stay with them, he went to Minneapolis, then a minor league team, where he was picked up by the White Sox in September of 1960. In 1963 the Reds, desperate for pitching, decided to take a gamble on him. Appearing in relief in 50 games, he finished with an ERA of 3.00. At the end of the season, the Reds demonstrated a sense of humor by giving him a pair of binoculars for his Christmas present! Al went on to pitch for the Minnesota Twins from 1964 to 1969. Between 1963 and 1968, Worthington was consistently among the top ten in game saves. After his playing days, he served as the Twins pitching coach from 1972 through 1973. In 1974 he signed on at Liberty University as their baseball coach and stayed with them until 1989, retiring as their Athletic Director.

" *The most important thing in life is to know that you are going to heaven when you die.* **"**

Letter from Al Worthington

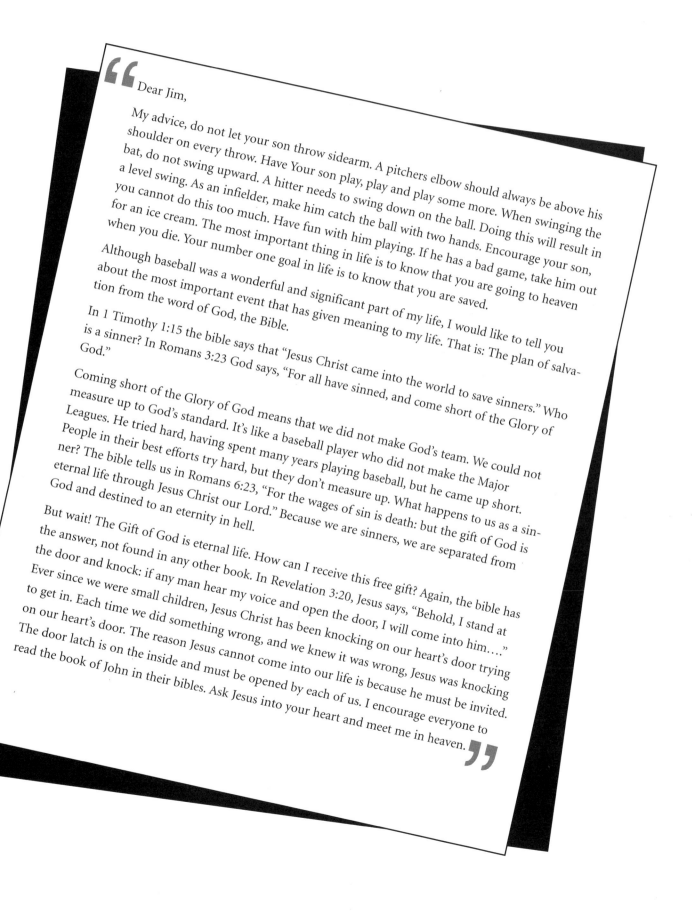

"Dear Jim,

My advice, do not let your son throw sidearm. A pitchers elbow should always be above his shoulder on every throw. Have Your son play, play and play some more. When swinging the bat, do not swing upward. A hitter needs to swing down on the ball. Doing this will result in a level swing. As an infielder, make him catch the ball with two hands. Encourage your son, you cannot do this too much. Have fun with him playing. If he has a bad game, take him out for an ice cream. The most important thing in life is to know that you are going to heaven when you die. Your number one goal in life is to know that you are saved.

Although baseball was a wonderful and significant part of my life, I would like to tell you about the most important event that has given meaning to my life. That is: The plan of salvation from the word of God, the Bible.

In 1 Timothy 1:15 the bible says that "Jesus Christ came into the world to save sinners." Who is a sinner? In Romans 3:23 God says, "For all have sinned, and come short of the Glory of God."

Coming short of the Glory of God means that we did not make God's team. We could not measure up to God's standard. It's like a baseball player who did not make the Major Leagues. He tried hard, having spent many years playing baseball, but he came up short. People in their best efforts try hard, but they don't measure up. What happens to us as a sinner? The bible tells us in Romans 6:23, "For the wages of sin is death: but the gift of God is eternal life through Jesus Christ our Lord." Because we are sinners, we are separated from God and destined to an eternity in hell.

But wait! The Gift of God is eternal life. How can I receive this free gift? Again, the bible has the answer, not found in any other book. In Revelation 3:20, Jesus says, "Behold, I stand at the door and knock: if any man hear my voice and open the door, I will come into him...." Ever since we were small children, Jesus Christ has been knocking on our heart's door trying to get in. Each time we did something wrong, and we knew it was wrong, Jesus was knocking on our heart's door. The reason Jesus cannot come into our life is because he must be invited. The door latch is on the inside and must be opened by each of us. I encourage everyone to read the book of John in their bibles. Ask Jesus into your heart and meet me in heaven."

Sam Chapman

SAM CHAPMAN 1938–41, 1945–51

NAME: Samuel Blake Chapman
BORN: April 11, 1916 Tiburon, CA
POSITION: Outfield
YEAR(S) IN MAJORS: 11 years
TEAM(S): Athletics, Indians
CAREER HIGHLIGHTS: All-Star 1946

Sam Chapman was an All American college football player for the University of California, and led the California Bears to a Rose Bowl victory in 1938. He was also an excellent baseball player and went directly from college to the Major Leagues. Starting with the Philadelphia Athletics in 1938, he played 11 years in the American League. He had speed, power, and a strong arm. An All Star in 1946, he hit 20 or more home runs five times, and in 1949, was in the league's top ten in total bases, home runs, RBIs and extra base hits. A popular player and team leader, Sam spent 1942 through 1944 as a Navy flier in World War II. As an outfielder, Chapman led American League outfielders in putouts four times, assists once, and errors twice.

" *To Nick,*
Practice—practice and have fun. "

Chapter 3

Bunting

Hal Naragon
Cleveland Indians

Ted Lepcio
Boston Red Sox

Tony Kubek
New York Yankees

Ed O'Brien
Seattle Pilots

Art Kenney
Boston Braves

Jim Davenport
San Francisco Giants

Bunting

Bunting

1 Every player should be willing to lay down a bunt if it can help their team. Baseball is one of the few sports that require a player to "sacrifice" him or herself for the team so you should know how to do it right. Bunting is a great tool in manufacturing runs.

2 Sometimes you may want to bunt for a hit, sacrifice a runner over into scoring position or "squeeze" a run home through bunting.

3 The best bunts are those that go about halfway down the base lines.

4 There are several ways to set up for a bunt, including the "square-around method" and the "pivot method." Whichever style of bunting you choose, there are several fundamentals which apply.

5 Bunting fundamentals:

- Keep the bat out in front of you and away from your body

- Make sure that you are bunting at a strike

- Let the ball hit your bat

- At the point of contact, try to catch the ball with your bat to cushion the contact and deaden the ball

- Start your bat at the top of the strike zone and bring it down to the ball

The Pivot Bunt

1 In the batter's box, move up so that your front foot is ahead of the plate just a little. This makes it easier to bunt the ball in fair territory.

2 Set up as you do in a normal batting stance. As the pitcher begins his stretch, pivot on the balls of your feet so that your hips and upper body face the pitcher. Don't lift your feet, just twist on your toes.

3 Keep your eyes fixed on the pitcher. Bend your knees slightly. Let your back leg take some of your weight.

The Pivot Bunt
Pivot on the balls of your feet so that your hips and upper body face the pitcher. Bend your knees slightly and extend your arms with a slight bend in the elbows.

Bunting

4 At the same time, slide your top hand up the barrel and re-grip the bat firmly using the thumb and the index finger. The other hand should stay in place by the knob of the bat. Tuck your fingers underneath. You don't want the ball hitting them.

5 You want to have your arms extended with a slight bend at the elbows.

6 Start the bat at the top of the strike zone and use your legs as an elevator to go up and down. The bat is started at the top of the strike zone for two reasons. First, the hitter is reducing the chance of bunting a pop-up by bringing the bat down to the ball. Secondly, if the pitch is above the bat, the hitter can pull the bat back and avoid bunting a bad pitch.

7 If you choose not to bunt the pitch, bring the bat back across the strike zone and return it to your shoulder. In the process, you are blocking the catcher's view for a split second. The catcher might lose sight of the ball and misplay it.

8 Angle the bat in the direction you want the bunt to go. Try to catch the ball on the fat part of the bat. Don't stab at the ball. This is why many bunts don't work. Avoid bad balls and high pitches. A good pitch to bunt is down in the strike zone. Since your bat is already at the top of the strike zone, if the pitch is higher than your bat, let it go (unless it is a squeeze play).

Square Around Method

1 Take the same position in the batters box as described for the pivot bunt. As the pitcher begins his windup, you actually turn in the batters box so that you are completely facing the pitcher.

2 This is accomplished by moving your front foot away from the plate and bringing your rear foot forward. Make sure that you do not step out of the batters box when you do this.

3 As you make your turn to face the pitcher, your top hand should be sliding up the barrel of the bat. Follow rules 3 through 8.

The Square Around Bunt
Move your front foot away from the plate and bring your rear foot forward.
Be careful not to step out of the batter's box.

Bunting

Drag Bunt

1 The purpose of the drag bunt is to get a base hit. Like the sacrifice bunt, it should only be used at certain times during the game.

2 The key element is to have your body in motion toward first base when you bunt the ball.

3 The successful drag bunt depends on the element of surprise, so disguise it as long as possible.

4 The only change you make is to move up in the box a little. Bunting the ball with your bat in front of the plate increases the chance of it being a fair bunt.

5 If you are a right-handed hitter, look to dump the ball down the third base line and if you are a left handed hitter, look to drag down the first base line or directly toward the second baseman.

6 If the first baseman is playing deep, the first base line may give the best opportunity of success.

Right-Handed Hitter

1 When attempting to drag bunt, pull your right foot back and move your right hand up the bat.

2 Place the bat in front of the body and the barrel pointed towards the pitcher. This provides the proper angle to bunt the ball down the third base line. By placing the bat in front of your body, you increase the chances of bunting it fair.

3 A common mistake in drag bunting is attempting to deaden the ball as you do in a sacrifice bunt. With a drag bunt, it's much more important to be accurate by bunting the ball down the line.

Left-Handed Hitter

1 For left-handed hitters, step back with your right foot toward the second baseman while moving your left hand up the bat and bringing the bat forward.

2 Point the barrel of the bat toward third base and be out in front of your body on contact. Look for a pitch from the middle of the plate in to bunt.

The Drag Bunt
The purpose of a drag bunt is to get a hit. Your body should be in motion toward first base when you bunt the ball.

Bunting

3 A common mistake is to cross over and try to get a great jump while bunting the ball. Again, bunting the ball accurately is more important than getting a great jump.

The Squeeze Bunt

1 The squeeze bunt is used in a close game to score a tying, go ahead, or insurance run.

2 It is most commonly used in the later innings, with a runner in third base and less than two outs.

3 The hitter and the base runner must work together for this play to be successful.

4 There are two types of squeeze bunts: the safety squeeze and the suicide squeeze.

Safety Squeeze

1 With the safety squeeze, the runner on third does not break for home unless he sees the bunt successfully laid down.

2 It is important that you lay down a bunt that the pitcher cannot field.

3 Either pivot or take a small step in order to quickly get into position to bunt. Do not show your intentions to bunt until the pitcher's arm comes forward and he cannot change the direction he is throwing.

4 Since the runner is waiting for a successful bunt, don't be afraid to take the pitch. Bunt the pitch either down the first or third base line. You may find that you want to go with the pitch or whatever side you are most confident bunting.

5 Make sure you don't try to get a good jump out of the box. Your job is to lay down a good bunt to score the man from third, not to get a base hit.

Suicide Squeeze

1 For the hitter, the suicide squeeze is much like the safety squeeze in that you must wait until the pitcher cannot change the direction of the pitch before you pivot to bunt.

2 It's much more difficult because the runner is not waiting to see if you have bunted the ball successfully before breaking from third. The assumption is you will bunt the ball no matter where it is pitched.

3 The runner from third must wait until the pitcher's arm is coming forward before making his break for home.

4 Unlike the safety squeeze where the location of the bunt is of primary concern, in a suicide squeeze, you want to make sure you bunt the ball fairly. It's very difficult for a team to defend against this play if the ball is bunted.

The Suicide Squeeze
The hitter must get the bat on the ball because the runner from third base is coming home.

Hal Naragon

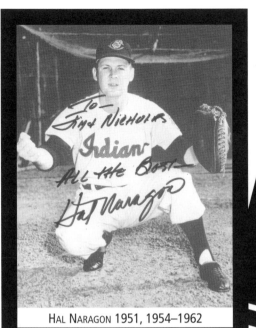

HAL NARAGON 1951, 1954–1962

NAME: Hal Naragon
BORN: October 1, 1928 Zanesville, OH
POSITION: Catcher
YEAR(S) IN MAJORS: 10 years
TEAM(S): Indians, Senators, Twins

Hal Naragon was born and raised in Ohio. At Barberton High School he played both basketball and baseball. With just a handshake, he signed on with the Cleveland Indians between his junior and senior year of high school and went to the minor leagues right after graduation. After appearing in just three games for the Indians, he was drafted into the Marine Corps. His first full year with the Indians was 1954 and he helped Cleveland to the American League Pennant and the team set a record for the most wins by an American League team (111). The New York Giants swept the Indians during the 54 World Series. A backup catcher for his entire career, he had the distinction of catching for 5 different "Hall of Fame" pitchers. In 1959 he was traded to the Washington Senators who later moved and became the Minnesota Twins. Naragon was the bullpen coach for the 1965 Twins when they won the pennant and was a coach for the Detroit Tigers in 1968, when they won the World Series.

My advice to Nicholas—Play as much as you can! Do a lot of throwing. Learn how to play the game mentally. Get a good education. Always believe in your dreams, and in yourself. Develop your natural abilities. Have fun and enjoy the game. Thanks for writing.

Ted Lepcio

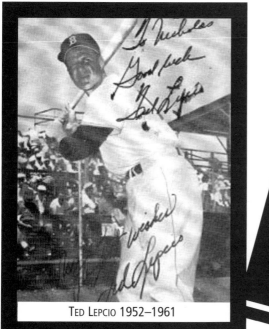

TED LEPCIO 1952–1961

NAME: Thaddeus Stanley Lepcio
NICKNAME: Ted
BORN: July 28, 1930 Utica, NY
POSITION: 2nd Base, 3rd Base, Shortstop
YEAR(S) IN MAJORS: 10 years
TEAM(S): Red Sox, Tigers, Phillies, White Sox, Twins

After graduating from Seton Hall University in 1951, Ted Lepcio was signed by the Boston Red Sox. In the spring of 1952, with just three months of minor league experience and four months prior to his 22nd birthday, Ted found himself playing 2nd base on opening day. The 22-year-old played for 10 seasons and on 5 different teams. Although his 1960 Phillies manager, Eddie Sawyer labeled him "the worst player I ever saw," he was a competent utility man with occasional power (15 home runs in 1956). Ted's strength was that he could play any infield position, which made him a valuable asset. He is one of only several players that has opened up a season in three different positions. His best year came in 1956 with the Red Sox when he hit 15 homers, drove in 51 RBIs, and ended with a .261 batting average.

> *Dear Jim, First and foremost, I was fortunate to have God-given talent to play. However I never wavered from the fact that the more educated you become, the better person you grow up to be. So I would stay in school for as long as I can. Play to the best of my ability and let the chips fall where they fall. Early in one's career it would be an advantage to play a few different positions until you find one in which you can excel. It gives you an appreciation and perspective of the game. It sounds like you and your son are on the right track. Good Luck.*

Tony Kubek

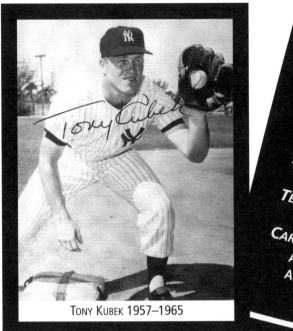

TONY KUBEK 1957–1965

NAME:
Anthony Christopher Kubek
BORN: October 12, 1936
Milwaukee, WI
POSITION:
Shortstop, Outfield
YEAR(S) IN MAJORS:
9 years
TEAM(S):
Yankees
CAREER HIGHLIGHTS:
All-Star 1958, 1959, 1961
A.L. Rookie of the Year 1957

Known as having defensive skills and the ability to make contact at the plate, Kubek first appeared on the Yankee roster as a utility ballplayer. He was the American League Rookie of the Year in 1957, spending time in the outfield, at shortstop, at third base, and hitting .297. Before long, Kubek became the everyday shortstop, and for eight seasons he and second baseman Bobby Richardson formed one of baseball's best double-play combinations, both on the field and at the plate. Tony appeared in six World Series with the Yankees. Playing in his home-town of Milwaukee, he hit a pair of homers in game three of the 1957 Series against the Braves. Injuries, especially to Tony's neck and back, shortened his playing career, but didn't stop him from being a three-time All-Star. After his retirement, Tony became the voice of NBC's "Game of the Week" and remains a very highly respected member of the baseball family. In 1987, he authored **Sixty-One, The Team, The Record, The Men**, chronicling the story of the New York Yankees' 1961 season. The book gave a player's insight to the inner workings of one of the great Yankee teams of all-time. During 1961 they won the World Championship and Roger Maris along with Mickey Mantle chased Babe Ruth's single season home run record, which Maris ultimately broke.

" *A young boy or girl should be taught the proper technique to avoid being seriously hurt . . .* "

Letter from Tony Kubek

" Dear Jim and Nicholas,

"The best suggestion I can give is to play (a lot). Catching, throwing, running and hitting helps to improve hand-eye coordination and develops the appropriate muscles to improve the skills that are necessary to play the game correctly. Self-discipline in the arena of sports and in life is an essential component for a happier, healthier, life style. I think too, that parents and coaches have to be careful to not over-coach. Let a youngster seek and find his or her own level without exerting too much pressure. Because the road to the Major Leagues is "reserved" for only a small percentage of those who play the game, it's important that Nicholas' priorities are molded properly by his parents and coaches:

1. His Lord and Savior
2. His family
3. His studies
4. His extracurricular activities. (Sports)

I'd like to add one specific thought regarding hitting. Too often I've heard parents or fans yelling at/to their young ones, as a baseball is propelled at them from the pitcher, "Let it hit you, it won't hurt you!" To me that's a big lie. IT DOES HURT! A young boy or girl should be taught the proper technique to avoid being seriously hurt when hit by a pitched ball.

Parents should practice with their kids and soft toss a rubber, sponge, tennis or wiffle ball right at him/her. Teach them to roll their front shoulder, for a right handed hitter, clockwise toward the catcher while tucking the head down to protect the face. They may get hit, but in the back where they are less vulnerable to serious injury. This also keeps them from "bailing out" or "stepping in the bucket." "Tucking" will help prevent the hitter from pulling the shoulder out and off the ball which leads to taking your eye off the ball. This is also an important step in learning to hit a curve ball. A Major League hitter has 2 fifths of a second, sometimes less, to decide all these things. We as parents should remember that Little Leaguers have this same challenge. I believe that this drill, repeated often, can help eliminate, as much as possible, the fears that can go with hitting and make for a better, more confident hitter. Stepping in the batter's box should be a challenging yet enjoyable experience whether one succeeds or not." "

Ed O'Brien

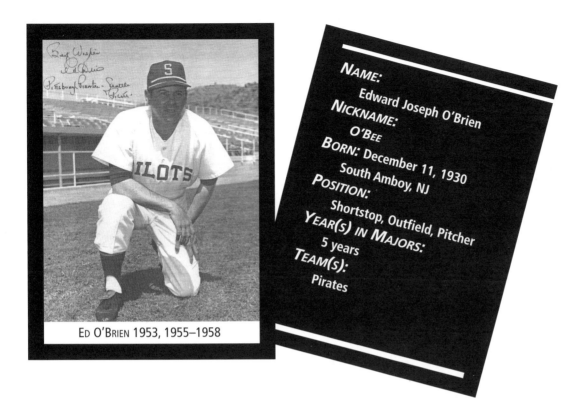

ED O'BRIEN 1953, 1955–1958

NAME:
Edward Joseph O'Brien
NICKNAME:
O'BEE
BORN: December 11, 1930
South Amboy, NJ
POSITION:
Shortstop, Outfield, Pitcher
YEAR(S) IN MAJORS:
5 years
TEAM(S):
Pirates

Branch Rickey signed Eddie O'Brien and his identical twin brother Johnny, to a bonus contract, to be Pittsburgh's double play combination. They both debuted in 1953, and were the first set of identical twins ever to play in the major leagues. When they took the field with Gene and George Freese in mid-1955, this marked the first time that two sets of brothers were playing on the same team at the same time. Both Eddie and Johnny also served in the military in 1954. During his time with the Pirates, Eddie was used as a shortstop, third baseman, second base-man, outfielder, and even a pitcher. The fun-loving brothers got great pleasure from confusing their managers, and the Topps Baseball Card company, as to who was who. In 1954, the Topps Company solved the problem by putting both of them on one baseball card. This was the first use of two players together on a modern card. When O'Brien left the Pirates in 1958, he became the athletic director at Seattle University and later was a coach for the 1969 Seattle Pilots.

" *Practice and play.*
Good Luck and Best Wishes "

Art Kenney

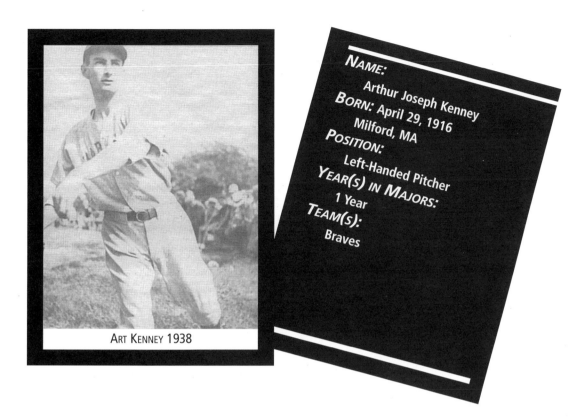

ART KENNEY 1938

NAME:
Arthur Joseph Kenney
BORN: April 29, 1916
Milford, MA
POSITION:
Left-Handed Pitcher
YEAR(S) IN MAJORS:
1 Year
TEAM(S):
Braves

Art Kenney grew up in Milford, Massachusetts, playing sandlot baseball during the 1920s. The hard throwing left-hander played ball in high school and moved on to Holy Cross College. He signed with the Boston Braves in 1938, after graduating from college, and appeared in 2 games for a total of 2 ⅓ innings. World War II cut his promising career short. Kenney spent four years in the Air Force and was stationed in England as part of the 398th Bomb Group. After the war, Art returned home and continued with his education. He went on to become a high school principal at several schools in the New England area for over 30 years.

Dear Nicholas,
To succeed in baseball, you must be in the best physical condition possible. No alcohol or drugs ever! Major League Baseball scouts have no interest in a prospect who uses alcohol or drugs. Keep up your interest and love for baseball. It's a great game.

Jim Davenport

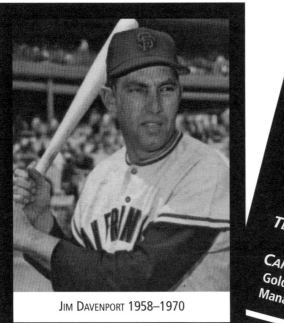

JIM DAVENPORT 1958–1970

NAME:
James Houston Davenport
NICKNAME:
Peanut, Golden Glove
BORN: August 17, 1933
Siluria, AL
POSITION:
3rd Base, Shortstop, 2nd Base
YEAR(S) IN MAJORS:
13 years
TEAM(S):
Giants
CAREER HIGHLIGHTS:
Gold Glove and All-Star 1962
Manager: 1985 Giants

With consistency, style, and versatility, Jim Davenport held down 3rd base for the Giants for 13 years. His first big league manager, Bill Rigney, called him "the greatest third baseman I ever saw." As a rookie in 1958, Jim quickly established himself as one of the National League's premier third basemen and hit .256 with 12 home runs and 41 RBIs. For the next three years (1959–1961) he led all National League third basemen in fielding percentage. In 1962, the Giants won the National League Pennant and Davenport won a Gold Glove Award and was selected for the All-Star team. In 1966, he established a major league record by playing 97 consecutive games (209 total chances) at third base without an error. After retirement, the Giants named Davenport the manager of their Triple AAA club in Phoenix, AZ. He also managed the Giants in 1985, and coached for the Padres, Phillies, Indians, and Tigers, extending his time around the major league scene for more than 40 years.

" *My advice to Nicholas is to keep working hard and give your best in what ever you are doing. I am sure someday he will look back and say, "I gave my best." And that is all he can do.* **"**

Chapter 4

Slumps

Chuck Hiller
San Francisco Giants

Bob Schmidt
New York Yankees

Bill Rogell
Detroit Tigers

Wade Boggs
Tampa Bay Devil Rays

Andy Seminick
Philadelphia Phillies

Roy Nichols
New York Giants

Bill Lee
Boston Red Sox

Slumps

Slumps

1. Did you ever notice that when you get into a slump, everyone wants to help? If you go two or three games without a hit, it seems that everyone has an answer for you. Your stance is wrong. Your bat is too heavy. Everyone seems to know the problem.

2. Sometimes it seems that the more advice you get, the worse you get. When in a slump, be careful about taking too much advice. Take advice only from those you trust. Look for simple solutions. Usually there are easy mechanical answers, such as starting the swing sooner or being more selective (swinging at strikes) Trust in yourself and your coach. Try to identify the problem and seek the simplest solution.

3. During the course of a season, failure will happen, so go easy on yourself. Even the great hitters in baseball go through slumps. A sign of a great hitter is the ability to fight through slumps. There is usually a mechanical reason why a hitter isn't hitting well. Sometimes slumps occur simply because of your mental approach. You can't be successful unless you first believe you can be successful.

Have A Plan

1. One way to gain confidence is to always go to the plate with a plan. Have an idea what you want to accomplish in each at bat. Are you going try to move the runner from second to third? Are you trying to lift a fly ball to score a runner from third?

2. Once you get to plate, clear your mind of any unnecessary thoughts and simply focus on the plan. Forget about what has happened in the past and concentrate on the present.

Get Back To Basics

1. Sometimes you can avoid a slump or pull yourself out of a slump by returning to the basics. Most slumps don't happen over night. It's usually a gradual process in which your timing starts to be a little slow or you begin swinging up on the ball.

2. If you feel yourself going into a slump, check your mechanics. Have someone watch you while you swing, check your Load and Stride, use the mirror and compare your swing with how you looked when things were going well. Most importantly, get some extra hitting practice.

Focus

1. An excellent way to maintain your focus is to use the "tunnel-vision technique." Pretend that there is a tunnel between the pitcher's delivery point and the hitting zone. Block out everything else. Direct all your attention toward this tunnel.

2. Prepare yourself to hit the ball when the pitcher's lead leg touches down and the ball emerges from the tunnel and approaches you. This can also improve your pitch selection.

3. If you can picture a tunnel that ends right at the strike zone, you probably won't swing at many bad pitches. So, focus before each at bat.

Slumps

Two Kinds Of Slumps

1 There different kinds of slumps that hitters go through. Some are simply numbers slumps. Sometimes you can have games in which you hit four line drives and each one happens to be right at a fielder. Does that mean you're in a slump? No, you're actually hitting well.

2 It's hard to convince yourself to ignore the numbers. If you believe in yourself and trust yourself, you will continue with the same mental approach even though the results aren't rewarding.

3 Some hitters think they need to start making adjustments because those line drives didn't translate into hits. If you are making good contact with the ball, you are hitting well, no matter if it's an out or a hit. Hitting a line drive or hitting a ball squarely is your goal. Don't confuse achieving your goals with achieving a particular batting average all the time.

4 The other kind of slump is when you just can't seem to get a hit no matter what you do. Most of the time you just hit weak ground balls and strike-out. In this kind of slump, your mechanics are probably out of whack, your swing is messed up, you're chasing bad balls, or your mental approach is poor. By the time you're 0-for-20, you suddenly believe you're never going to get another hit. This is a *real* slump that you need to address. Just know the difference.

Success Can Cause Slumps

1 Sometimes success can cause a hitter to fall into a slump. A hitter becomes so confident in his hitting ability because he is cranking every pitch thrown at him. Suddenly he believes he can hit anything. The hitter then starts swinging at balls out of the strike zone. And it's easy to figure out what happens next.

2 Once a hitter starts swinging at balls out of the strike zone, his swing starts to fall apart. This is the type of slump that a coach should be able to spot quickly. And fix quickly. Be aggressive at the plate and be confident. But be selective. Swing at strikes. Remember: The best swing in the world can't hit a bad ball.

Set Simple Goals

1 When you're trying to break out of a slump, set simple goals to begin with. Go into a game with a small goal such as getting a base hit. After a few games, you may tell yourself that you want to hit two balls hard. This promotes confidence. Slowly, as you continue to reach your goals, you will begin to believe in yourself again. Instead of the negative thoughts, you begin to think you're capable of succeeding again.

2 Remember that slumps can be painful but they can also make you stronger. The ability to fight through a slump can make you a better overall hitter. It helps you to grow as a ball player and prepares you for future slumps. Once you get through one slump, you can always tell yourself you can get through another.

Chuck Hiller

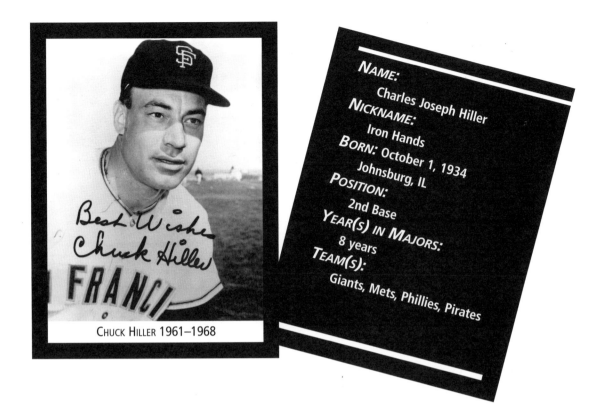

CHUCK HILLER 1961–1968

NAME: Charles Joseph Hiller
NICKNAME: Iron Hands
BORN: October 1, 1934 Johnsburg, IL
POSITION: 2nd Base
YEAR(S) IN MAJORS: 8 years
TEAM(S): Giants, Mets, Phillies, Pirates

Chuck Hiller played eight seasons in the majors, all in the National League. Nicknamed "Iron Hands," he led National League second basemen with 29 errors in 1962, but also helped the Giants to the league title. The Yankees went on to beat the Giants in the World Series, capped by a 1–0 victory in game seven at Candlestick Park. During that series, Hiller became the first National League player to hit a World Series grand slam, connecting off Marshall Bridges in the seventh inning of game four. Later used extensively as a pinch hitter by the Mets, he led the league with 15 pinch hits in 1966. After his playing days were over, Chuck worked for the Kansas City Royals organization. He was a Royals' coach from 1976–79 and was part of manager's Whitey Herzog's teams that lost in the American League Championship Series to the Yankees in 1976, 1977, and 1978.

> *Be good at schoolwork first and the game second. Practice, Practice, Practice, and have a great deal of fun doing it all the time. I don't think that any of us thought we would be Major League players at a young age. Good luck to you and Nick.*

Bob Schmidt

BOB SCHMIDT 1958–1963, 1965

NAME:
Robert Benjamin Schmidt
BORN: April 22, 1933
St. Louis, MO
POSITION:
Catcher
YEAR(S) IN MAJORS:
7 years
TEAM(S):
Giants, Reds, Senators, Yankees
CAREER HIGHLIGHTS:
All-Star 1958

As a rookie in 1958 with the San Francisco Giants, Schmidt won the catchers job and would stay there for the next several years. Although he batted only .244, he came on strong during the early part of the year and finished with 14 home runs and led National League catchers in double plays. He won a spot on the National League all-star team as a rookie and set a since-broken record with 22 putouts in one game. Traded to Cincinnati in 1961, and then to the Washington Senators in 1962, Bob was used mostly as a backup catcher. He finished up his playing days with the Yankees in 1965.

" *You must practice as much as possible. Best Wishes to you and Nick.* "

Bill Rogell

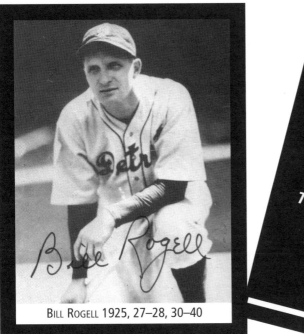

BILL ROGELL 1925, 27–28, 30–40

NAME:
William George Rogell
BORN: November 24, 1904
Springfield, IL
POSITION:
Shortstop, 2nd Base, 3rd Base
YEAR(S) IN MAJORS:
14 years
TEAM(S):
Red Sox, Tigers, Cubs

Born in 1904 and orphaned at the age of 11, Rogell grew up on the south side of Chicago. In 1910 he dropped out of school and found work anywhere to help support his younger brothers. After playing semipro ball for several years, Bill came up to the big leagues with the Red Sox in 1925. Poor hitting sent him to the minor leagues several times. In 1929 he signed with the Detroit Tigers and became their regular shortstop throughout the 1930s.

A talented shortstop with a strong arm, he and Charlie Gehringer made up one of the most solid double play combinations in the game. In 1934 he helped the Tigers win their first pennant in 25 years. He was one of four Tigers with 100 or more RBI's. A tough but popular player, Bill had his fair share of scrapes including a throw he made during the 1934

World Series. In game 4, Rogell relayed the ball toward first base for a double play and hit pitcher Dizzy Dean in the head. Dean went down and was out cold, but it was reported in the next day's newspapers that, **"X-rays of Dean's head showed nothing."** The Tigers lost the World Series to St. Louis that year, but were back to win the World Series in 1935 over the Cubs. During the 1930s, Rogell was among the leagues top 10 in fielding 3 years, assists 2 years, games played 3 years, stolen bases 3 years, walks 2 years, doubles and triples 1 year each. After his baseball career ended, Rogell had a long, successful career as a Councilman for the city of Detroit from 1942 to 1980. At the time he offered this baseball advice, Rogell is one of the oldest living Major League Baseball players.

Letter from Bill Rogell

" Jim,

Your question is hard to answer. I do not know your boy, how big he is and if he is willing to work hard. There's a lot of ups and downs in the game of baseball. He's got to build himself up. Don't overdo it, but stick to it.

I don't know what position he would like to play, but he should get a rubber ball and bounce it off a wall and then field it bare-handed. This will develop what they call, "soft hands." Then progress to the glove.

Hitting is something he has to pick up by himself. Never give up! You're as good as the pitcher. You can fail to hit him, say three times at bat, but there's always the fourth time up. I hope that I have helped you and I also hope that your son plays the outfield. Do not be a pitcher. I love to watch the young players, not the super-stars of today. Good luck to you both for a second successful book. "

Bill Rogell

Wade Boggs

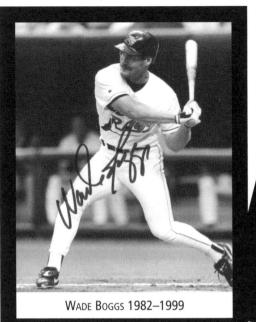

WADE BOGGS 1982–1999

NAME:
Wade Anthony Boggs
BORN: June 15, 1958
Omaha, NE
POSITION:
3rd Base, Outfield, DH
YEAR(S) IN MAJORS:
18 years
TEAM(S):
Red Sox, Yankees,
Devil Rays
CAREER HIGHLIGHTS:
All-Star 12 times
Golden Glove 1994, 1995
AL Batting Title 5 times

An all-state kicker on the football team for Tampa's, Plant High School, Wade Boggs was not considered much of a prospect in the minors. During his rookie year with the Red Sox in 1982, he booted the first two ground ball that were hit to him. But after getting his first major-league hit on April 26th, he set the American League on fire with a .349 average. In his 18-year career, he reached base safely in 80% of his games and was the only batter in the twentieth century to have seven consecutive 200-hit seasons. He appeared in twelve All-Star games as a third baseman. In the seven years between 1982 and 1988 he batted .349 or higher six times. Between 1983 and 1996 he was an All-Star 12 times, and was in the top ten in: Batting Average 11 times, Hits 9 times, Doubles 8 times, and Walks 9 times. In 1996, ten years after Boston's loss to the Mets in the World Series, Boggs found himself back in the World Series with the Yankees. When the Yankees clinched the series after Game 6, Boggs led the team in its victory lap around Yankee Stadium on horseback, courtesy of the NYPD. Wade spent his last two seasons with the Tampa Bay Devil Rays. He hit the first home run in Devil Rays history and, on August 7, 1999 with a home run to right field, he achieved his 3000th hit. The future Hall-Of-Famer retired after the 1999 season.

> **There are no shortcuts, you must work hard and practice as much as possible.**

Andy Seminick

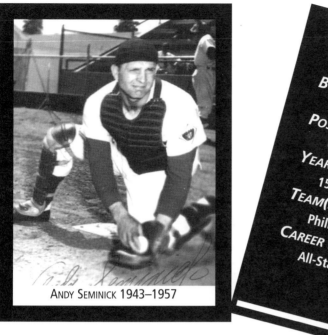

ANDY SEMINICK 1943–1957

NAME:
Andrew Wasil Seminick
BORN: September 12, 1920
Pierce, WV
POSITION:
Catcher
YEAR(S) IN MAJORS:
15 years
TEAM(S):
Phillies, Reds
CAREER HIGHLIGHTS:
All-Star 1949

Andy Seminick had the desire to get away from the coal mines of West Virginia, where his father worked, and enough talent to play in the majors for 15 seasons. At age 23, after playing three years of Class-D ball in the Appalachian League, Seminick was with the Philadelphia Phillies for the last three weeks of the season. He became the Phillies' first string catcher from 1946 through 1951 and again in 1955, after four years with the Reds. In 1949, he racked up 24 homers and 68 RBI's and earned a spot on the All-Star team. The following year, Andy put up identical numbers and helped the Phillies to their first pennant since 1915. Playing hurt during much of his career, he suffered an ankle injury late in the 1950 season. Determined to finish up the season and play in the World Series against the Yankees, Seminick kept the injury quiet. After the Phillies lost the series, he discovered that he had been playing with a broken ankle. After retirement in 1957, Andy became a Phillies coach, scout, and minor league manager. In 2002, at the age of 81, he was still attending spring training camp as an instructor.

Have good habits in keeping a strong body. Also strong hands, and strong arms. This will help you to have a strong throwing arm. You have to be dedicated to being a ball player.

Roy Nichols

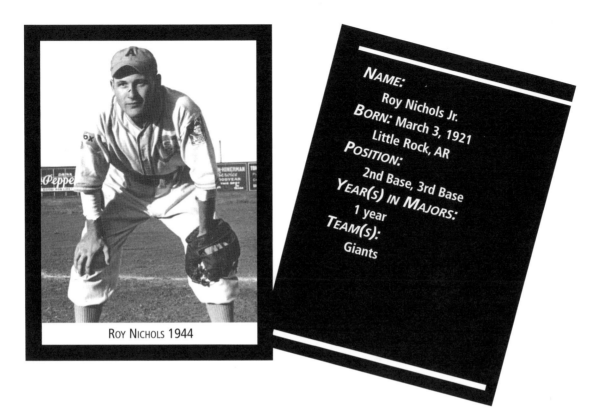

ROY NICHOLS 1944

NAME:
Roy Nichols Jr.
BORN: March 3, 1921
Little Rock, AR
POSITION:
2nd Base, 3rd Base
YEAR(S) IN MAJORS:
1 year
TEAM(S):
Giants

Although Roy Nichols spent 12 years in baseball, his only stint in the Major Leagues was 11 games with the New York Giants in 1944. He began his baseball career at age 18 and played in the North Carolina and the International Leagues. Plagued with back problems, he became a player/manager with the Cambridge (MD) Dodgers in 1947. Roy went on to manage the Johnstown (PA) Johnnies, under the Dodgers system for three more years, leading them to the Mid-Atlantic Pennant in 1949. Considered one of Branch Rickey's favorite managers, he was a talented defensive player with a good baseball mind. After retiring from baseball, Nichols had a successful career in sales and management for 32 years with the Pittsburgh Plate Glass Company. Roy's uncle, Bill Baker, was a catcher for the Cincinnati Reds.

> *I was offered $100.00 per month, for 5 months, to play baseball. I jumped at the chance.*

Letter from Roy Nichols

"Dear Jim,

Thanks for your note. I hesitate to offer advice concerning your son. Times are so much different now. When I played my first year, I was 18 years old – depression time, no jobs—just graduated from high school. Scholarships to college were practically nonexistent then. I was offered $100.00 per month, for 5 months, to play baseball. I jumped at the chance. Now, kids have so many options. If he has exceptional talent, running, throwing, strength, hand and eye coordination, well – if I were in his shoes and had the burning desire to play, I would probably try for the gold ring. However, knowing what I know and looking backward, I would try to prepare an option in the event it turned sour after 1 or 2 years. I played with 2 fellows that were Dentists. Another was a jeweler. Don't put all your eggs in one basket.

My only son became a musician. He played Little League, had good size and very good strength. But talent for baseball—no. After 6 or 7 years at Syracuse University he changed jobs and went to LA University (Monroe). He has been on the teaching staff there for 19 years. If I had pushed him into baseball, I truly believe he would have failed. Music has been his love and his life.

If you truly love the game and qualify—OK. But find a second choice, that he really cares for and prepare for it. I saw many players with Major League talent fizzle out after a year or two. It is not an easy life. It's better now, than in my day. I played eleven years. After baseball I went to work for PPG Industries for 32 years and this was my retirement. Good Luck to you and your son."

Roy Nichols

Bill Lee

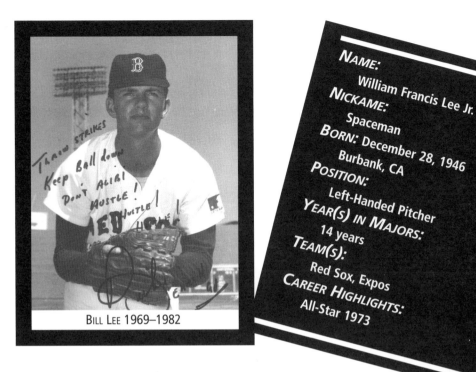

BILL LEE 1969–1982

NAME:
William Francis Lee Jr.
NICKAME:
Spaceman
BORN: December 28, 1946
Burbank, CA
POSITION:
Left-Handed Pitcher
YEAR(S) IN MAJORS:
14 years
TEAM(S):
Red Sox, Expos
CAREER HIGHLIGHTS:
All-Star 1973

Bill Lee is one of the most colorful personalities that baseball has ever seen. It is said that he earned the nickname "Spaceman" when, on his first view of Fenway Park's left field wall called "The Green Monster", he asked, "Do they leave it there during games?" The left-hander pitched for 14 seasons with a career record of 119–90. Between 1973 and 1975 he had three consecutive 17-win seasons with the Red Sox, and in 1979 he won 16 games with the Montreal Expos. Always willing to speak his mind, he once stated: "I hate the designated hitter, and all the other wrinkles that have been introduced in an attempt to corrupt the game. I wanted to go back to natural grass, pitchers who hit, Sunday doubleheaders, day games, and the nickel beer . . . Baseball is the belly button of America. If you straighten out the belly button, the rest of the country will follow suit." He was known as a pitcher with great control. He was an all-star in 1973 and between 1973 and 1979 he was in the top ten in ERA twice, complete games twice, and shutouts twice.

> *Nick, You need to Hustle, Hustle, Hustle, all the time. If you are a pitcher, throw strikes, keep the ball down, and don't make excuses. Work hard. Hitting a curve ball is one of the hardest things to do in baseball. Be patient at the plate. You are like a soldier, in the middle of a battle, with fast balls coming at you left and right. You have to determine when the time is just right, and then jump on it.*

Chapter 5

Hitting Drills

Whitey Kurowski
St. Louis Cardinals

Spider Jorgensen
Brooklyn Dodgers

Woody Jensen
Pittsburgh Pirates

Billy Hunter
New York Yankees

Johnny Sain
Boston Braves

Frank Fanovich
Philadelphia Athletics

Hal Jeffcoat
Chicago Cubs

Mike Naymick
St. Louis Cardinals

Hitting Drills

Quick Hands Drill

1 The **purpose** of this drill is to develop quickness in your swing and build up hand and arm strength. You will need 8 to 10 baseballs, a bat, and a partner. For best results, use a fence, tarp or net.

2 The batter should get into his/her regular stance about 5 feet from the fence or net.

3 The partner should face the batter on one knee, with the baseballs arranged for easy access.

4 When the batter is in the ready position, the balls are tossed up into the batters strike zone.

5 The batter swings at each ball and then brings the bat back to the ready position as quickly as possible. When returning to the ready position, the bat should follow the same path that was used to make contact with the ball.

6 The partner should then toss another ball, getting into a rhythm with the hitter. The time between each toss should be very short.

Get into your regular batting stance,
about 5 feet from a fence or net.

Have your partner face you
and toss the balls into your strike zone.

Make Contact!

Finish and then bring the bat back to the ready
position quickly, using the same path.

Hitting Drills

Bat to the Belly

1 The **purpose** of this drill is to develop a short "inside out" swing that takes the bat quickly to the ball by using a wall, net or fence. This drill emphasizes that a hitter must rotate the hips ahead of the hands and pull the knob of the bat through the hitting zone before extending the arms in front of home plate.

2 The hitter should stand, with a bat, facing a fence. Place the knob of the bat against your belly and then move forward so that the other end of the bat lightly touches the fence. Take your normal batting stance at this distance from the fence. Practice your swing without hitting the fence with the end of the bat.

3 Increase the speed as the swing becomes more comfortable. (Be careful not to damage the bat or the fence during this drill.)

3 Developing a compact swing is one of the most important elements of hitting a baseball. By eliminating all unnecessary movement in the swing, a hitter is able to get the head of the bat into the hitting zone quicker. A shorter swing will make a hitter more successful against faster pitching. It will also increase bat control and allow the hitter to make solid contact instead of grounding out hitting a weak pop-up.

4 A hitter should always keep his lead arm bent at about 45 degrees until he makes contact. Both arms should be extended at contact, but if the lead arm extends too early in the swing it will result in a long, slow swing.

5 Hitting the wall or fence with the bat means that you are extending the arms too soon. To bring the hands through the strike zone first, take a normal step as if to swing, and "throw" the end of the handle through the strike zone. Finish high and over the front shoulder, your belly button facing the imaginary pitcher. This will increase bat speed and help you to hit the ball harder.

Stand with a bat, facing a fence. Take the bat and put the end against the fence lightly. The end at the handle should make slight contact with your belly. Now take the normal batting stance at that distance from the fence and take about ten or fifteen swings. If the bat is making more than light contact with the fence, you're not bringing your hands through first. Notice how the hips open and back foot twists during the swing.

Hitting Drills

Top Hand/Bottom Hand

1 The **purpose** of this drill is to develop better balance and mechanics. Balance means having your weight centered over the middle of your body. Mechanics means hitting the ball using the proper technique. You will need a bat, a ball, and a batting tee. A fence, tarp or net is optional but helpful.

2 Get in a comfortable stance in front of the tee. A batting tee should always be set up approx. 6 inches in front of the batter's front foot. (Batters should always hit the ball in front of the plate, not over the plate)

3 Stand at the tee as if you're going to hit a baseball. Your feet are a shoulder-width apart

4 Take a swing. Note that each arm makes a different motion. If right handed, your right arm makes a punching motion down and out. The left hand makes a karate chop from your shoulder to the tee.

5 There's nothing wrong with "choking up" on the bat handle, or positioning your hands higher up on the bat handle, whatever is comfortable for you.

First one arm . . .

1 Work each arm separately. First, hold the bat in your front arm. (The one that faces the pitcher) Grab the front of your shirt with the other hand. This will help you keep a proper balance.

2 Now slice your hand down toward the tee at a 45 degree angle, karate style. Remember that your other hand must hold onto the front of your shirt. Try to keep a nice level swing through the strike zone.

3 Don't worry about where the ball goes. Try to hit the ball in the middle, not on top or the bottom.

. . . Then the other arm

1 Now do the drill for your back arm. Make your front arm hug your chest while making a punching motion toward the tee with your rear hand. Drive your bat down and out. Remember to keep a level swing through the strike zone.

For the Top Hand/Bottom Hand drill, hold the bat in your front arm. Grab the front of your shirt with the other hand. Now slice your hand down toward the tee at a 45-degree angle, karate style. Now do the drill for your back arm. Make a punching motion toward the tee with your rear hand. Drive your bat down, through, and then out of the strike zone. Try to keep a nice level swing.

Hitting Drills

Using a Batting Tee

1 This section will teach you some simple drills using your batting tee and how to hit pitches over different areas of the plate. Hitting off a tee is one of the best ways to work on and develop the proper swing. Since there is no pitcher and the ball is stationary, the swing itself gets the full attention.

2 You can practice using both hands in the swing or using only the top or bottom hand only. Also you can vary the tee location to simulate an inside or outside pitch. When hitting off of a tee, try to hit ground balls and line drives right up the middle of the field. If you can continuously make solid contact and put the ball down the middle of the field, then you are on your way to improvement.

3 To practice hitting the ball to the opposite field, place your tee on the outside (back edge) of home plate. Stand next to the plate and make contact following your normal swing. Don't try to hit a home run, line drives are what you want. Home run power can come later.

4 To practice hitting the ball up the middle, move your tee to the front of home plate. This time, when you hit the ball it should head straight out to center field.

5 To practice pulling the ball, place the tee on the inside edge of home plate. Try to "pull the ball." If you're batting right-handed, you're standing on the left side of home plate and the ball should be going to left field.

6 Try using Wiffle Balls or rolled up socks if your space is limited

Place your tee to the front of home plate. Try to drive the ball straight up the middle of the field.

Place your tee on the outside of the plate. This will help you to hit outside pitches (Hit to the opposite field)

Place your tee on the inside of the plate. This will help you to hit inside pitches. (Pull the ball)

Hitting Drills

Chair Drill

<u>1</u> The **purpose** of this drill is to develop a proper path to the ball. It also corrects upper-cutting and is an excellent drill for developing a "line drive" stroke.

<u>2</u> Place a batting tee on home plate, with a folding chair behind the tee, with the seat part closest to the tee.

<u>3</u> Make sure that the tee is just slightly lower than the back of the chair so that you must swing with a slightly downward angle and then level through the ball.

<u>4</u> If you uppercut, you will only hit the back of the chair.

<u>5</u> Metal chairs seem to be very effective in teaching the proper bat angle during the swing.

<u>6</u> For a change, place a batting tee on the inside half of the plate or the outside half of the plate.

Deflated Basketball

<u>1</u> The **purpose** of this drill is to force you to focus on really driving all the way through the swing, otherwise the ball doesn't go anywhere.

<u>2</u> This drill includes using a slightly deflated basketball on the tee. You want just enough air out that when pushed in the ball will "slowly" return to round.

<u>3</u> Place a plunger in the tee upside down (plunger part facing up) and place a deflated basketball on top of the plunger and practice hitting the basketball. Try to hit the ball level (around chest high) into a hitting net or wall.

<u>5</u> This drill will help increase your power at the point of impact. Remember to swing smoothly, knob of the bat through the strike zone first, using your wrists to whip the bat through the strike zone.

Place a chair behind the batting tee. This will prevent you from swinging up on the ball. It will also give you a "line drive" stroke.

Hit a deflated basketball off the batting tee. Get a plunger and place it upside down in the batting tee. Practice driving the ball all the way through your swing.

Hitting Drills

Hip Twists

1 The **purpose** of this drill is to get your lower body working correctly without thinking about it. The lower body part of the swing is essential for balance and power.

2 Place a broom handle behind your back on the waistline. With hands gripping the broom handle from behind, get in a stance next to the batting tee. Take your inward turn, stride and attempt to hit the ball on the batting tee.

3 As you take your stride toward the ball, use your top hand (right hand for right handed hitter and left hand for left handed hitter) and forcefully pull the broom handle around with your waist, rolling up on back foot (squashing the bug) and with your head down, toward the batting tee.   Make sure that you take a comfortable stride and keep your weight on your back foot. Don't lunge.

4 Knees and belly button should then be facing the "pitcher."   Go back to normal stance and repeat.

Fence Drill

1 The **purpose** of this drill is to develop a compact swing. It helps to prevent the hitter from opening up (extending the arms) too soon. You will need a bat and a wall or fence.

2 The hitters should stand in the ready position with their rear foot about 12 to 14 inches from the wall or fence.

3 Practice your swing by bringing your hands and the knob of the bat down and through the strike zone.

4 If the bat is hitting the fence, you need to shorten up your swing.

5 Extending the arms too soon will result in a slow swing. This is sometimes seen when hitters wave the bat as they wait for the pitch, or with hitters that have a "hitch" in their swing. A "hitch" is when hitters actually drop the arms and bat and then bring them up to the ready position just before they swing.

Use a broom handle and batting tee and develop your lower body motion.

Fence Drill

Hitting Drills

Ball Drop Drill

1. The **purpose** of this drill is to develop quickness and a compact swing. It forces you to bring your hands straight to the ball.

2. You should set up about 5 feet from a fence or net, just as in the "Quick Hands" drill. A partner should set up facing you. If desired, your partner can stand on a chair or crate.

3. Your partner is going to drop the baseballs into your hitting zone from a point above your head.

4. The partner should be in a position to avoid being hit by the bat, but still be able to drop the ball into your strike zone. If possible, have your partner yell out, "chest," "waist," or "knees" and then try to make solid contact with the ball in each of those areas.

Knob to the Ball Drill

1. The **purpose** of this drill is to practice bringing your hands through the strike zone first. When a hitter swings at a pitch, the hands and knob of the bat should come through the strike zone first, toward the ball. The barrel of the bat will follow, in a whip-like motion, giving the hitter added power.

2. Like many of the other drills, the knob to the ball drill will help develop "muscle memory." When practiced, the hitter will instinctively bring the hands to the ball with a short compact swing.

3. Stand in your normal position at the plate. Have your partner "soft toss" balls to you. Load and stride toward the ball, bring the knob of the bat through the strike zone and try to hit the ball with the knob of the bat. Be sure to include your lower body action in the drill.

Have a partner drop balls into your hitting zone from a point above your head.

Practice bringing the knob of the bat through the strike zone toward the ball.

Hitting Drills

Batting Cages

1 Batting cages are a great place to practice hitting, especially for kids who have to contend with cold weather and snow in the fall, winter and spring months.

2 The controlled atmosphere allows for quality hitting without the hassle of chasing baseballs all over a field. You have balls being pitched at you just like in a game, so you can work on your timing.

3 The machines will let you pick what speed you want the pitches thrown at and can be adjusted high, low, inside, or outside.

4 Another good thing about batting cages is you usually don't have a coach correcting everything you do, so you can experiment a little and just have fun.

Live Hitting

1 Live hitting is probably the best practice situation for any player. The **purpose** is to allow the hitter to put all of the mechanics into motion.

2 It is most effective when you simulate a game situation as much as possible. You should do this outside, against a pitcher throwing off the mound and a catcher calling the balls and strikes.

3 In a live practice, the pitcher should be trying to get the hitter out. This allows the hitter to practice under pressure.

4 Remember that every time you swing the bat you should have a purpose in mind. You can do this by creating situations for yourself. Simulate a hit and run by having an imaginary runner on 1st base and trying to hit the ball on the ground somewhere. Move that same runner to 3rd base by trying to hit the ball to the right side of the field. Try to bring that runner home with a fly ball to the outfield.

5 Live hitting also gives you a chance to work on any problems you might be having with your swing. For example, if you are hitting a lot of fly balls, maybe you are swinging up on the ball and if you can't seem to catch up with the fastball, you might want to work on your load and stride.

Live hitting is the number 1 practice tool.

Hitting Drills

Soft Toss

1 The **purpose** of the Soft Toss drill is to practice the proper swing mechanics such as stance, load stride, and the swing. It allows a hitter to concentrate on the fundamentals without the pressure of live pitching.

2 You will need a partner, a bucket of balls, and a pitcher's net. The hitter should take his position at the plate.

3 The pitcher's net is set up between home plate and the pitcher's mound. (About 30 to 40 feet from home plate) Your partner then tosses the balls into the strike zone.

4 This is a good drill to practice hitting the ball in those areas that give you the most trouble.

Wiffle® Ball

1 Wiffle Ball is the most popular practice tool for young baseball players. Games can be played in the back yard or driveway. Make up your own rules.

3 Hang a wiffle ball on a string from the rafters in the basement or the garage and practice hitting it.

4 Practice hitting by using a batting tee and a bag of wiffle balls. Tee it up and start swinging. Try to hit the wiffle ball cleanly off a tee. The more you practice, the sooner you will become a better hitter. If you are alone, use a regulation bat, toss a wiffle ball up in the air and practice hitting it.

Toss-Up

1 The **purpose** of the Toss-Up drill is to practice the proper swing mechanics and to help develop hand-eye coordination.

2 You will need a partner, a bucket of balls, and a bat. The hitter should take his position at the plate. Have your partner field the fly balls and grounders.

3 Hold the bat in your back hand and a ball in your front hand. Toss the ball up so that it passes through your strike zone on the way down. After you toss the ball up, grip the bat with both hands and swing.

4 Practice hitting fly balls. Try hitting grounders to all areas of the infield.

Have a partner toss pitches into your strike zone.
Use a protective net.

Use a Wiffle Ball and bat in your yard for fun and practice.

Find an empty field and practice "Toss-UP" with a friend.

Whitey Kurowski

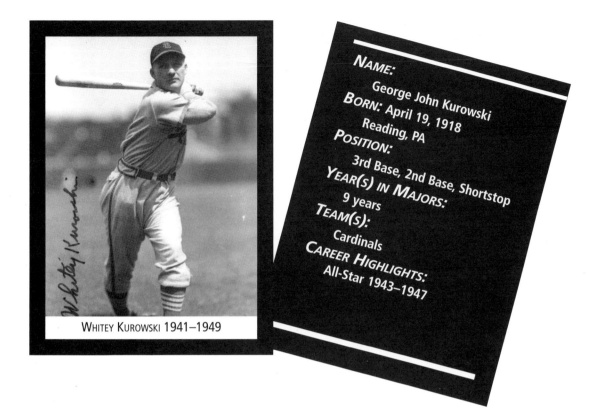

WHITEY KUROWSKI 1941–1949

NAME:
George John Kurowski
BORN: April 19, 1918
Reading, PA
POSITION:
3rd Base, 2nd Base, Shortstop
YEAR(S) IN MAJORS:
9 years
TEAM(S):
Cardinals
CAREER HIGHLIGHTS:
All-Star 1943–1947

Whitey Kurowski joined the St. Louis Cardinals at the end of the 1941 season and stayed with the team for his 9 Major League seasons. A stocky infielder with surprising speed, he overcame childhood Osteomyelitis (which made his right arm shorter than his left) to become one of the finest third basemen of the 1940s. Steady and reliable, he hit 20 or more home runs three different seasons and batted .300 or better his last three full seasons. In the field, he led the National League three times in putouts, twice in fielding average, and once each in assists and double plays. Whitey played in the 1942, 1943, 1944 and 1946 World Series. A five-time All Star, he was the hero of the 1942 series: tripling in the second game to give the Cards a 3–0 lead, scoring the winning run in game 3, driving in two runs to lead the Cards to victory in game 4, and slamming a ninth inning, three-run homer in the fifth game that won the world championship over the New York Yankees.

"Listen to your coaches. Practice hard at all times. Do not give up. Play hard, but learn all the time. Best Wishes."

Spider Jorgensen

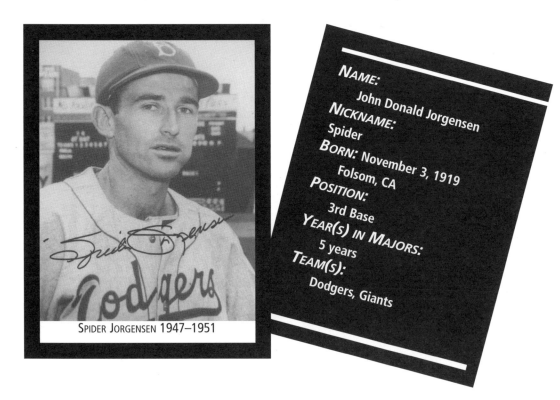

SPIDER JORGENSEN 1947–1951

NAME:
John Donald Jorgensen
NICKNAME:
Spider
BORN: November 3, 1919
Folsom, CA
POSITION:
3rd Base
YEAR(S) IN MAJORS:
5 years
TEAM(S):
Dodgers, Giants

As a rookie in 1947, the wiry Jorgensen was the Dodger's clutch third baseman. He recorded his best season that year, when he appeared in 129 games with 121 hits and 67 RBIs, helping the Dodgers to the National League Pennant. The Dodgers lost the World Series to the Yankees that year in 7 games. He was the starting third baseman in Jackie Robinson's first game, and continued with the Dodgers until 1950, when he was traded to the Giants in mid-season. He completed his major league career in New York in 1951, after bruising his throwing arm while hunting that winter and injuring it further in spring training. Spider was with the 1951 Giants when Bobby Thomson hit his famous home run to defeat the Dodgers and go on to the World Series against the Yankees. He was acquired by Oakland in the Pacific Coast League in the 1950s and was a strong defensive element in the Oaks' infield for several years. In 1996 Jorgensen was inducted into the Brooklyn Dodgers Hall of Fame.

"Learn how to relax. There are many courses that you can take to learn how. What you have to do is make your nerves work for you in a positive way rather than a negative way. In other words, "nervousness can be just what I need to make me a winner." It took me a long time to make them work for me in a positive way.

Woody Jensen

WOODY JENSEN 1931–1939

NAME:
Forrest Docenus Jensen
NICKNAME:
Woody
BORN: August 11, 1907
Bremerton, WA
POSITION:
Outfield
YEAR(S) IN MAJORS:
9 years
TEAM(S):
Pirates

Woody Jensen began his Major League baseball career in 1931 with the Pittsburgh Pirates. The 24 year-old played for 9 seasons on one team and ended his big league playing career in 1939. In the mid-1930s, Jensen teamed with Paul and Lloyd Waner in the Pittsburgh outfield. He was called "Woody," as a play on Forrest, and because he once played in the Timber League. The left-handed hitter rarely walked and set a ML record with 696 at-bats in 1936, batting leadoff with Lloyd dropping to second. In 1935 he was ninth in the majors with a .324 average and third in total hits with 203. During the 1936 season Woody was in the league's top ten in games played, at bats, hits, and doubles.

> **Stay away from alcohol and drugs. Practice always. Play to win, but know how to accept the losses.**

Billy Hunter

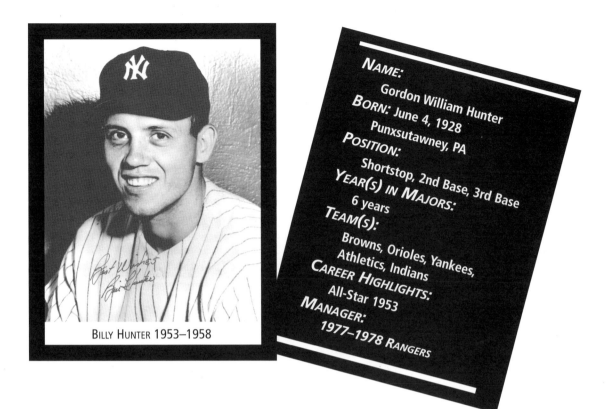

BILLY HUNTER 1953–1958

NAME:
Gordon William Hunter
BORN: June 4, 1928
Punxsutawney, PA
POSITION:
Shortstop, 2nd Base, 3rd Base
YEAR(S) IN MAJORS:
6 years
TEAM(S):
Browns, Orioles, Yankees,
Athletics, Indians
CAREER HIGHLIGHTS:
All-Star 1953
MANAGER:
1977–1978 RANGERS

Billy Hunter began his Major League Baseball career in 1953 with the St. Louis Browns. The 25 year-old played for 6 seasons on 5 different teams and ended his big league playing career in 1958. A flashy fielder, Hunter was an All-Star as a Browns' rookie. He was hitting .252 at the time, but finished the season at .219. He was with the Yankees in the 1955 and 1956 World Series. The Yankees lost to the Brooklyn Dodgers in 1955, but beat the Dodgers in the 1956 series highlighted by Don Larsen's perfect game performance. In 1977 and 1978 Billy managed the Texas Rangers finishing in second place both years. As the Orioles' third base coach, he was renowned for his frantic, arm-wheeling "Go!" signal.

> *Play as much as you can. Play at levels that force you to keep improving, in order to keep playing. Best wishes.*

Johnny Sain

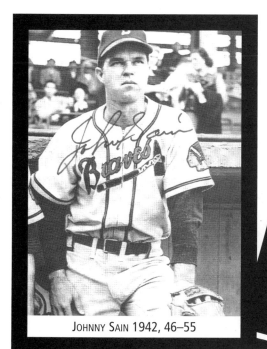

JOHNNY SAIN 1942, 46–55

NAME:
John Franklin Sain
BORN: September 25, 1917
Havana, AR
POSITION:
Right-Handed Pitcher
YEAR(S) IN MAJORS:
11 years
TEAM(S):
Braves, Yankees, Athletics
CAREER HIGHLIGHTS:
ALL-STAR 1947, 1948, 1953
LEAGUE LEADER IN WINS 1948

Johnny Sain has been called, "one of the greatest pitching coaches that ever lived." This statement refers to the influence he had on such pitchers as Denny McLain, Wilber Wood, Jim Perry, and Whitey Ford, during his 14 years as a pitching coach. This may be true, but it is Sain's pitching career that distinguishes him the most. A rookie in 1942 with the Boston Braves, he spent 1943 through 1945 in the service. Upon his return he won 20 or more games four times between 1946 and 1950. In 1948 he led the league in wins with 24, helping the Braves reach the World Series. During that 1948 season fans would chant, "Spahn and Sain and pray for rain," meaning that the Braves could win it all, with just Warren Spahn and Johnny Sain, and a day off because of rain. His Major League credits include: 9 World Series appearances, 4 as a player (Braves and Yankees) and 5 as a coach, 3 All-Star games, pitching nine complete games in 29 days in 1948, and striking out only 20 times in eleven years. As if this weren't enough, Johnny has the distinction of being the first pitcher to face Jackie Robinson in the majors, and the last pitcher to face Babe Ruth in an organized game (1943).

> *If I could have planned my whole life, it couldn't have been any better. But without the adversity I faced, I don't think it would have meant as much today. I was released four times from class D ball and I didn't have good speed on my fastball and people wondered about my ability. Because I wasn't fast, I had to learn how to throw a variety of breaking stuff, with different speeds and motions. Baseball is a tough game, but that made me want to do it even more.*

Frank Fanovich

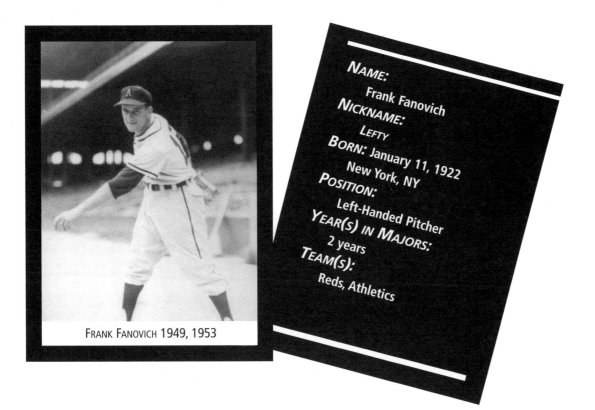

FRANK FANOVICH 1949, 1953

NAME:
Frank Fanovich
NICKNAME:
LEFTY
BORN: January 11, 1922
New York, NY
POSITION:
Left-Handed Pitcher
YEAR(S) IN MAJORS:
2 years
TEAM(S):
Reds, Athletics

A sandlot player in his native New York City, Frank Fanovich never played High School baseball. During World War II he played ball for the Army, eventually becoming a player-manager before going overseas. At the end of the war, a friend arranged for Frank to meet with the New York Giants organization. He was signed to a minor league contract and sent to Jacksonville, Florida. Although he spent over 10 years in organized baseball, Fanovich only reached the Major Leagues for two years. Signed by the Cincinnati Reds in 1948, they brought him up to the majors in 1949. After being signed by the Philadelphia Athletics he saw time in the majors again in 1953. Used by both clubs as a relief pitcher, he failed to record a win or save in his two Major League seasons. At the end of his baseball career, Fanovich became a patrolman for the City of New York. The last 10 years of his career were spent with the Manhattan North narcotics squad. He was fondly known as the "Voice of Delta Base."

" To become a good baseball player, you will need two qualities. Extreme dedication, and a love for the great game of baseball. "

Hal Jeffcoat

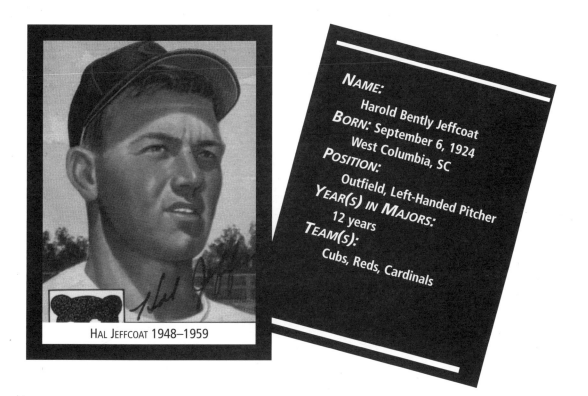

HAL JEFFCOAT 1948–1959

NAME: Harold Bently Jeffcoat
BORN: September 6, 1924
West Columbia, SC
POSITION: Outfield, Left-Handed Pitcher
YEAR(S) IN MAJORS: 12 years
TEAM(S): Cubs, Reds, Cardinals

The fast, smooth-fielding Jeffcoat debuted with the Chicago Cubs in 1948, playing in 134 games, hitting .279. From 1948 until 1953, he played in the outfield. During the 1954 season, he provided the baseball community the equivalent of a career change. Despite his fielding ability, his light hitting led the Cubs to suggest that he try pitching. He made the conversion and became one of the top relievers in baseball at the time. In his first season on the mound, he finished at 5–6 with a 5.19 ERA in 104 innings pitched. In 1955, however, Jeffcoat improved to 8–6. Traded to the Reds in 1956, his next two seasons would prove to be his most productive as a pitcher. He finished 8–2 in 1956, and was 12–13 in 1957. Hals' older brother George pitched in the National League.

> *Nick, Enjoy the game. Play and practice as much as you can. Listen when advice is given. Live a clean and spiritual life. Education is a must and should come first. Try hard not to neglect it. Plan a useful career for the future, when the game is over. Finally enjoy what you do and stay healthy. Good Luck.*

Mike Naymick

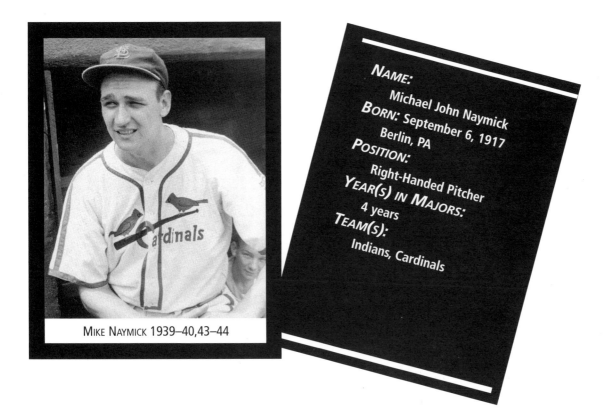

MIKE NAYMICK 1939–40,43–44

NAME:
Michael John Naymick
BORN: September 6, 1917
Berlin, PA
POSITION:
Right-Handed Pitcher
YEAR(S) IN MAJORS:
4 years
TEAM(S):
Indians, Cardinals

Since baseball was not offered at Wierton High School in West Virginia, the tall, lanky Naymick played both football and basketball. After high school, Mike played ball for the Weirton Steel Company where a scout spotted him and sent him to the Cardinals for a tryout. He was later signed by the Cleveland Indians and was brought up to the majors in 1939. He was used mainly as a spot reliever bouncing between the majors and the minor leagues. As World War II approached, Mike was eager to serve. He enlisted and passed his physical but was considered too tall. They had no clothes (6' 8") or shoes (17½) to fit him. After baseball, Naymick went to work for the Parsons Corporation and was head of the Q.A. department.

> *Tell your son to finish school and to make his education a priority. Be good to your health and take care of your body. No drugs, alcohol, etc. Always stretch and stay limber. This will be the best way to prevent injuries. Diligence is the key. Play from the heart. Be a diverse player and work on all your skills equally. Home runs should not be your goal. Increase cardio-vascular endurance, especially if you are a pitcher. Being able to bunt is also a great skill to have. Most importantly, be a team player.*

INDEX

B
Baker, Bill 58
BALANCE DRILL, THE 6
BALL DROP DRILL 68
BATTING CAGES 69
BATTING GRIP, THE 4
BAT SELECTION 6
BATTING TEE 65
BAT TO THE BELLY 63
Berra, Yogi 17
Blanchard, Johnny 17
Boggs, Wade 56
Bridges, Marshall 52
BROOMSTICK DRILL 67
Brown, Mace 20
BUNTING 37, 38

C
Carlton, Steve 28
CHAIR DRILL 66
Chapman, Sam 36
CLOSED STANCE, THE 5
Coscarart, Pete 33
COUNT, THE 26
COUNT, THE 0–0 26
COUNT, THE 3–2 26

D
Dark, Alvin 18
Davenport, Jim 48
Dean, Dizzy 54
DEFLATED BASKETBALL DRILL 66
Delsing, Jay 12
Delsing, Jim 12
DRAG BUNT 40

F
Fanovich, Frank 76
FENCE DRILL 67
Fisk, Carlton 28
Freese, George 46
Freese, Gene 46

G
Gutteridge, Don 16

H
HAVING A STRATEGY 23
Hiller, Chuck 52
HIP TWISTS 67

Hitchcock, Billy 30
HITTERS COUNT, THE 27
HITTING DRILLS 61
HITTING FUNDAMENTALS 2
Hopp, Johnny 14
Howard, Elston 17
Hunter, Billy 74

J
Jeffcoat, Hal 77
Jensen, Woody 73
Jorgensen, Spider 72

K
Kenney, Art 47
Kindall, Jerry 32
KNOB TO THE BALL DRILL 68
KNOWING THE OTHER TEAM 22
KNOWING THE PITCHER 24
KNOWING THE UMPIRE 25
Kubek, Tony 44
Kurowski, Whitey 71

L
Larsen, Don 74
Lee, Bill 60
Lepcio, Ted 43
LIVE HITTING 69
LOAD 7
Lucadello, Johnny 31

M
Mantle, Mickey 17, 31, 44
Maris, Roger 17, 44
MECHANICS OF THE SWING 1
MENTAL ASPECTS 22
MENTAL ASPECTS OF HITTING 21
Mize, Johnny 14
Mueller, Ray 16

N
Naragon, Hal 42
Naymick, Mike 78
Nichols, Roy 58

O
O'Brien, Ed 46
O'Brien, Johnny 46
OPEN STANCE, THE 5

P
Pilarcik, Al 29
PITCHERS COUNT, THE 27
PIVOT BUNT, THE 38
POSITIONING THE BAT 6

Q
QUICK HANDS DRILL 62

R
Richardson, Bobby 44
Rickey, Branch 46, 58
Rigney, Bill 48
Robinson, Jackie 72, 75
Rogell, Bill 54
Ruth, Babe 20, 44, 75

S
SAFETY SQUEEZE 41
Sain, Johnny 75
Sandlock, Mike 11
Sawyer, Eddie 43
Schang, Wally 31
Schmidt, Bob 53
Seminick, Andy 57
Skowron, Bill 17
SLUMPS 49, 50
SOFT TOSS 70
Spahn, Warren 75
SPECIAL BATTING SITUATIONS 10
SQUARE AROUND BUNT 39
SQUARED STANCE, THE 2
SQUEEZE BUNT 41
STRIDE 8
STRIKE ZONE, THE 2
SWING, THE 9
SUICIDE SQUEEZE 41

T
Thomson, Bobby 18, 72
TOP HAND/ BOTTOM HAND 64
TOSS-UP 70

W
Waner Lloyd 73
Waner Paul 73
WIFFLE BALL 70
Wise, Rick 28
Worthington, Al 34
WORKING THE COUNT 26

MY AUTOGRAPHS

MY AUTOGRAPHS

MY AUTOGRAPHS

WRITE TO A PLAYER
ASK FOR AN AUTOGRAPH OR PHOTOGRAPH

ANAHEIM ANGELS
Angel Stadium of Anaheim
2000 Gene Autry Way
Anaheim, CA 92806

ARIZONA DIAMONDBACKS
Bank One Ballpark
401 East Jefferson Street
Phoenix, AZ 85004

ATLANTA BRAVES
Turner Field
755 Hank Aaron Drive
Atlanta, GA 30315

BALTIMORE ORIOLES
Oriole Park at Camden Yards
333 West Camden Street
Baltimore, MD 21201

BOSTON RED SOX
Fenway Park
4 Yawkey Way
Boston, MA 02215-3496

CHICAGO CUBS
Wrigley Field
1060 West Addison
Chicago, IL 60613-4397

CHICAGO WHITE SOX
US Cellular Field
333 West 35th Street
Chicago, IL 60616

CINCINNATI REDS
Great American Ball Park
200 Main Street
Cincinnati, OH 45202

CLEVELAND INDIANS
Jacobs Field
2401 Ontario Street
Cleveland, OH 44115

COLORADO ROCKIES
Coors Field
2001 Blake Street
Denver, Colorado 80205

DETROIT TIGERS
Comerica Park
2100 Woodward Avenue
Detroit, MI 48201

FLORIDA MARLINS
Pro Player Stadium
2267 Dan Marino Blvd.
Miami, FL 33056

HOUSTON ASTROS
Minute Maid Park
501 Crawford, Suite 400
Houston, TX 77002

KANSAS CITY ROYALS
Kauffman Stadium
1 Royal Way
Kansas City, MO 64129

LOS ANGELES DODGERS
Dodger Stadium
1000 Elysian Park Avenue
Los Angeles, CA 90012

MILWAUKEE BREWERS
Miller Park
One Brewers Way
Milwaukee, WI 53214

MINNESOTA TWINS
Metrodome
34 Kirby Puckett Place
Minneapolis, MN 55415

MONTREAL EXPOS
Olympic Stadium
4549 Avenue Pierre de Coubertin Ave.
Montreal, Quebec H1V3N7

NEW YORK METS
Shea Stadium
123-01 Roosevelt Avenue
Flushing, NY 11368-1699

NEW YORK YANKEES
Yankee Stadium
Bronx, NY 10451

OAKLAND ATHLETICS
Network Associates Coliseum
7000 Coliseum Way
Oakland, CA 94621

PHILADELPHIA PHILLIES
Citizens Bank Ballpark
1 Citizens Bank Way
Philadelphia, PA 19148

PITTSBURGH PIRATES
PNC Park
115 Federal Street
Pittsburgh, PA 15212

ST. LOUIS CARDINALS
Busch Stadium
250 Stadium Plaza
St. Louis, MO 63102

SAN DIEGO PADRES
Petco Park
100 Park Boulevard
San Diego, CA 92101

SAN FRANCISCO GIANTS
Pac Bell Park
24 Willie Mays Plaza
San Francisco, CA 94107

SEATTLE MARINERS
Safeco Field
First Ave. S. & S. Atlantic St.
Seattle, WA 98104

TAMPA BAY DEVIL RAYS
Tropicana Field
One Tropicana Drive
St. Petersburg, FL 33705

TEXAS RANGERS
The Ballpark at Arlington
1000 Ballpark Way
Arlington TX 76011

TORONTO BLUE JAYS
Skydome
1 Blue Jays Way, Suite 3200
Toronto, Ontario M5V1J1

Be sure to include a self addressed stamped envelope so they can mail it back to you.

Hey Dad, Wanna Get Another Copy?

HEY DAD, WANNA PITCH TO ME?

ISBN 0-9746272-0-8
96 pages
$12.95

Everything that a future big league hitter needs to know.

—Rick Dumont , *The Cabinet Press*

Buy Both
for $24.95
Save $3.00

HEY DAD, WANNA PLAY CATCH?

ISBN 1-884186-14-9
152 pages
$14.95

I see only one potential problem with the book being purchased by a baseball-loving family. A glove-toting youngster, after finishing the book asks, "Hey Dad, Wanna Play Catch?" A book-toting father answers, "Sorry, son, I'm reading."

—Joe Sullivan, *Manchester Union Leader*

✂ -

Name_____

Address_____

City_____ State_____ Zip_____ Country_____

Hey Dad, Wanna Pitch To Me? _____copies at $12.95 = $_____

Hey Dad, Wanna Play Catch? _____copies at $14.95 = $_____

Shipping & Handling: $_____
$5.00 for first book, add $1.50 for each additional book

BEST VALUE!
Order One of Each Book and Save! _____sets at $24.95 = $_____

Shipping & Handling: $_____
$5.00 for each set

Total $_____

Payment Options:

CHECK or **MONEY ORDER**:

Mail this form with payment to:
Hollis Publishing
95 Runnells Bridge Road
Hollis, NH 03049

CREDIT CARD ORDERS:

For payment by credit card, please visit:
www.amazon.com
www.bn.com (Barnes and Noble)
www.hollispublishing.com
www.heydad.org

VOLUME DISCOUNTS:
Phone 800.635.6302 for volume rates.